SWORD OF FAITH

SWORD OF FAITH

A true story of one man's struggles when
he is caught between the battles of demons
and angels in the world of dreams.

WAYNE LOUIS

Sword of Faith

A true story of one man's struggles when he is caught between the battles of demons and angels in the world of dreams.

iUniverse books may be ordered through booksellers or by contacting:

iUniverse
1663 Liberty Drive
Bloomington, IN 47403
www.iuniverse.com
1-800-Authors (1-800-288-4677)

ISBN: 978-1-4917-4217-4 (sc)
ISBN: 978-1-4917-4218-1 (e)

Library of Congress Control Number: 2014913963

Printed in the United States of America.

iUniverse rev. date: 08/18/2014

Sword of Faith
Note from the Author

I have tried to recreate events, locales and conversations from my memories of past events. In order to maintain their anonymity in some instances I have changed the names of individuals and places, I may have changed some identifying characteristics and details as to protect people depict in this book. This book is designed to provide recounts of events that occurred based on the author memories to my readers. It is sold with the understanding that the publisher is not engaged to render any type of psychological, legal, or any other kind of professional advice. The content of this book is the sole expression and opinion of its author, and not necessarily that of the publisher. No warranties or guarantees are expressed or implied by the publisher's choice to include any of the content in this volume. Neither the publisher nor the author shall be liable for any physical, psychological, emotional damages or incidents that could occur from reading this book. Our views and rights are the same: You are responsible for your own choices, actions, and beliefs.

Acknowledgments

Special thanks to my wife, who let me spend many hours on the PC writing this story. Her enduring patience will forever be remembered. I've not done all things right, but finding her after making such a bad choice the first time is only proof that there is goodness left in this world. I've never told her about this, so I am sure when she reads this book she will have questions, too!

Last, but not least, thanks for the patience of my dog Scooter. When I first started writing this book he couldn't stay in the room with me. I too could feel their presence! There were nights during my writing that he would stand in the hallway barked at the air. My wife could not understand why. One night during my writing of this book Scooter was so upset that he had to sleep with us. You see, Scooter was a fifty-eight pound dog. Scooter was so upset that he wanted to lay on me. I do not think Scooter had my protection in mind as he climbed into our bed for his safety.

Preface

This is one man's true story of a life time of dreams where he is caught in battles between demons and angels.

CONTENTS

The Introduction

Let me begin by going back to a time when I was really young. Looking back, it seems so long ago. I wish I could forget those memories yet I can't. Some memories will never die. Like all children I had bad dreams and my mother told me it was nothing. What if that wasn't true? What if my dreams were real? I had my share of bad dreams when I was young. They were bad. So bad, to this day, I have never forgotten them.

My dreams were filled with monsters. They were so vivid that, after I had awakened, I was afraid to look out from under my covers. It wasn't just a dream, it was happening. I found comfort in writing this book. Why? I believe that there's more to some dreams than merely the things our mind filters through at night while we sleep. There are messages in our dreams. If only we remember them. I know that I am not the only one who ever had a message from a dream.

I believe these messages were coming from angels. Yes, angels. But these were not the only messengers. No, there were others. I received messages from demons as well. In fact, most of my messages were coming from demons. In this book, I will tell you about my dreams.

My purpose is to let others know that at night there may be a monster behind that knock at your door. If not, you are lucky and pray that you never do. I believe there are others having these dreams, maybe they will have them this very night. They are terrified to sleep for fear of what their dreams will bring. I hope that reading this book will provide them some understanding they are not crazy. It can happen to anyone.

I cannot say dreams are real as we grasp reality. I do believe that there is a realm where the world of dreams exists. What happens there is just as real as what happens in our world while we are awake. I do believe what happened in my dreams did happen in a lower realm where some never go or don't remember. It is not a blessing or a curse, but a few of us have the ability to travel between the realm of dreams, a place where there is a distinct line between this world and the world spirits, demons and angels interact with us.

I know many religions believe dreams provide a way for the angels to send messages. Who is to say that angels and demons don't visit us in dreams? In the Bible, God's messages were often told in dreams by angels. Many times angels came to men in dreams in both the Old Testament and the New Testament.

There are three types of dreams. The first type of dream is the most common. Dreams about work, home, family, love, good times and bad. Very few people ever have the second kind of dream. They are the good dreams where an angel comes to comfort or to give us a message. The third type of dream is a curse, where one goes into the realm of dreams where demons and evil spirits exist.

My story is based on my true-life memories of dreams. I have changed the names to shield my family. My memories of past dreams began when I was around six years old. It was over forty years ago yet these are the dreams I can never forget.

CHAPTER 1
IN THE BEGINNING THERE WERE DREAMS

"Be careful what you wish for; it just might come true" - unknown

My dreams began when I was very young. I still have faint memories of dreams from my early childhood. This is a time when I should have been dreaming of dump trucks and sand boxes. Or perhaps playing with toys or running in the yard. But no, my dreams were of monsters. I did a lot of running in my dreams as I was being chased. Yes, chased by real monsters.

I'm sure that many have had a bad dream especially when they were little. Children have bad dreams. And we have all dreamt of monsters. However, for most children they will wake up when the monster gets too close to them. In my dreams, I would get caught by the monsters and I didn't wake up. I was forced to fight the monsters because I couldn't wake up!

This was a constant chain of dreams for me, a small boy who grew up in a small town, in Tennessee. These were not the kind of dreams children usually have. I tried to tell my mother many times, but she would always just say they were just bad dreams. I am sure that other children have had this happen to them. Your mother, father, big brother or big sister would say it was just a bad dream. They don't mean anything. Go back to sleep.

I do not agree. It was not just a bad dream. There are dreams much more than a bad dream. As I tell this story, you too will understand why some dreams are not bad dreams, they are nightmares.

A dream I had when I was about five or six years old still haunts me. I slept in the same room with my sister in bunk beds. The beds were not stacked together. My bed was on the far side of the room. My sister's bed was closest to our bedroom door. One night I heard something under my bed. The noise woke me up, so I moved to the edge of my bed and looked down at the dark floor. It was very dark at first, but there was a window on the wall between our beds. A little amount of light was beaming through the window and onto the floor.

I got up on all fours in my bed and slowly looked down. All I could see was the hardwood floor. I carefully leant forward just a little more to get a better angle to see if the sound could be coming from under my bed. Without warning, a claw flew out from under my bed. It was so fast that I did not have time to move out of its reach!

This claw locked onto my wrist and starting pulling me down under my bed. It frightened me so bad that I screamed. I was fighting with all my might, but whatever had my arm was stronger than me. I could see my sister lying in her bed. I screamed for her to help me. I called her name, but she just lay in her bed asleep.

I was almost pulled off the bed by this time. I couldn't understand why my sister would not wake up and help me. I was so scared that I started crying and all of a sudden I felt the claw loosen on my hand. I knew this was my chance. I jerked my arm as hard as I could! I could feel the claws tearing my flesh from my wrist and down my hand as it came loose for the steel grip. I knew that just one last jerk and my hand would be free!

The motion of pulling my wrist free threw me back in the bed. My body fell backward and my head hit the wall on the other side of the bed. I woke up and I was too frightened to move. After a couple of seconds, I slowly crawled under the covers and did not move until I fell asleep.

I still carry with me this fear of looking under the bed at night.

My nights were filled with dreams of monsters. When I was about seven I had a dream that change things for me. It's strange now after all these years how the details seem so clear. I was running through an old brick building. I believe it was some kind of warehouse, yet I had never been in a warehouse at that time in my early life.

A big monster with huge claws was chasing me. Like so many details in dreams you just know and in this dream I knew about the monster. Like so many other dreams I had not seen the monster but I knew it was there. I could see in the distance a light shining at the far end of a room. I was running fast and the monster was getting closer and closer. I could feel the monster's breath on the back of my neck that sent chills throughout my body. This spurred me to run even faster. I ran towards the light at the far end of the room.

As in most of my dreams I'm not sure why I did not simply stop and hide. I was running down what seem to be an aisle where there were large wooden beams rising from the floor. The wooden beams disappear into the darkness of the ceiling. All I was thinking was just run, run fast, no run faster. There were smells in this old warehouse. One smell was the strong odor of tobacco and I could smell it each time I inhaled. That smell filled my nose and mouth with each breath. And there was the smell of old wood. The smells were strange yet I knew what they were. I can still smell them now by just thinking about that dream.

Some things are burned into my memory forever. I remember the desperation as I looked down that endless room. There in the distance I could barely make out a glimpse of light at the end of the room. I could hear the monster's footsteps getting closer and closer. I darted for the light in a ray of hope. As I got closer, I could make out a light glowing through the window. I had been running forever and at times I felt so small! And then I felt a faint glimmer of hope.

I allowed myself to imagine there might be a way to escape the monster. I knew that I would not wake up until this dream was ready to let me. I didn't have control in my dream. I ran up to the window and grabbed ahold of the wooden boards that lined the opening. The wood was rough in my small hands as I leaned through the opening. I was wondering, why wasn't there any glass in the window? So many things did not make sense. Especially when you are a little boy being chased by a monster.

I leaned out to see if I could jump. When I looked out I realized that the window was several stories high. The longer I looked down, the higher the window became. There was no way I could jump. The outside walls were made of brick. As I looked up, the brick walls disappeared into the clouds. The clouds were gray and scary.

I felt all hope was lost and a new kind of fear took hold of me! The fear of being trapped. Then it hit me, this was a dream! I could not wake up. I leaned out the window again looking for some way to escape. I was scared to death as I was being gripped by fear. I knew that I had to do something or the monster would have me any second.

I thought if I only had claws then I could climb the brick wall. Suddenly, claws started growing where my fingers and toes had been just seconds before. There was no time to waste. I crawled out on the windowsill and started climbing my way up the brick wall. I could feel my claws digging into the brick. There was a power that manifested within me. I found I could will my claws to dig into the hard brick wall. Even more amazing was the fact that my new set of claws could support my weight on the side of the brick wall.

I had climbed way up the wall before I remember the monster. I looked down and the monster was climbing out of the window and onto the wall. Again, panic hit! I had not thought about the possibility that the monster might be able to fit through that window. It was very small even for me to climb through. How did this big monster fit through that window? I would later learn the laws of physics do not apply in dreams. And I had forgotten for just a second that it had big claws too! Worse yet, its claws were bigger and better at climbing the wall.

I climbed, faster and faster. But then I began to slow down. Digging into the brick was hard. I had to think about what I was doing. I had to draw on the power within me to dig my claws into the hard brick. I could not keep climbing up for much longer as I was tiring fast. I was climbing as fast as I could, but the monster was stronger. It was climbing as if the wall was as easy as walking. I knew the monster was gaining on me. I remember looking down with the feeling of panic. I knew the monster was only seconds from reaching me.

Just then my luck ran out, the monster grabbed my ankle! I could not pull loose from that steel grip. I could feel its claw digging into my skin. The monster started to laugh as it started to pull me back down the wall. My grip in the brick started to loosen. I struggled with all my strength, but I was running out of strength and will power.

All of a sudden, I reached deep within myself and found the power to begin digging at the brick on the side of the wall with one of my claws. Large sections of bricks started breaking loose from the wall where I was hanging on with my other three claws. Somehow I knew this was my only hope! I tore harder into the brick with my free claw. Then a large section of the brick that had been supporting me and the monster broke away from the wall.

We were both falling, but the monster had not let go of my ankle. I looked down past the monster, but I could not see any bottom to our fall. Then in a desperate act of self-preservation, the monster let go of my ankle. The monster was trying it's best to grab hold of the brick wall. I grabbed with both of my claws and dug into the brick on the side of the wall. I smacked the wall so hard that it almost knocked the breath out of me. Somehow I managed to hold on for dear life. In the last few seconds, I managed to look down to see the monster being swallowed by the darkness below. I could hear its howls long after it had disappeared in the blackness. Then I woke up.

As I look back I wonder how it was that no one seem to know about my dreams. Yet, we see abuse happen all the time to children and no one seems to really see it. Often what happens is the abuse becomes the norm. And the person who is being abused just accepts that the abuse as a normal way of life. I didn't talk about my dreams because who would have believed me?

This was the kind of dreams I had off and on during my early childhood. I have always wondered if others had dreams like this when they were little. Still after many years I remember my dreams as if they happened only last week. I don't believe that these are ordinary dreams. No, these were dreams that allowed things from the spirit world to enter into my dreams. My Dreams did not end like most of childhood dreams that only happen once in a blue moon, no they occurred almost every night!

One Saturday afternoon when I was sixteen, I was watching a movie and got a crazy idea. When we are young and foolish we get all types of ideas. At the time, most of these ideas sound good but far too often we live to regret those ideas. I was laying on the sofa in our living room. We had just moved into a cabin style house only a few miles outside of Cookeville, Tennessee. My father was in the construction business and he liked building houses with different designs. He would think of new, unique designs and then build the house out of a simple drawing he made. Most of the designs were in his head and not on paper. Often he would build a house, and then he would like it so much that instead of selling it, we would move in for a while. He would eventually get tired of the house, put it up for sale, and we would move again. It wasn't so bad for me, because we always stayed in the general area around town.

The house had a bedroom in the basement which was my bedroom, and I thought was very cool. I had my own bathroom next to the laundry room. What I really liked was the door leading outside from the family room. I could come and go without my parents knowing about my timing. As a sixteen year old, this was a dream come true. My father had built a desk and bookshelves in the wall next to my bedroom closet, a style of that time. The room was paneled with the ever so popular white pine. The closet had a set of double wooden slatted doors that pulled open on a track, very upscale for the time.

There was an old monster movie on TV. The movie focused on a professor who had spent his life fighting demons. The Professor said, knowledge is the real tool of power. This got my attention and the gears in my young head began to turn. My idea was that I could become knowledgeable just like the professor. I then could take on the demons that had tormented me for years. I was still having dreams with monsters, but now I had realized that they were not monsters, but real demons. As a teenage I felt like most teenagers, indestructible. That wasn't true, I just lacked the wisdom and knowledge that comes with age.

I have a sister who was taking some college courses at Tennessee Technical University. I got her to agree to take me to the library on campus. I did not tell her of my plan as she may not have agreed to help. I was looking for books on demonology. I was surprised to find several books on demonology in a small college in the middle of the Bible belt. I thought luck was on my side that night. Maybe it was luck, maybe it was fate playing me. Fate put my sister in the right spot to aid me in getting my hands on books that I would have been better off not reading.

My sister didn't even look at what books I gather up for her to check out for me. She was too busy flirting with a guy at the Library's desk. There was something about seeing my older sister flirting with a guy that made me want to give up girls forever. I knew that I had to endure the pain of this moment if I wanted the books. Now with my tools of knowledge, I set out to be the greatest demon fighter the world had ever known! There is an old saying that I'm sure everyone has heard. *"Be careful what you wish for; it just might come true."*

So, for the first three nights I sat reading and making notes from the books. I could not believe all the information on demons I was finding between the covers of these books. I read late into the night as I could not put the books down. But it was on the fourth night that everything changed.

I had just finished studying for the night and closed the books. I set them in a neat pile, each reference book on top of the other. I went through my usual routine of getting ready for bed. Then I crawled into bed and lay down.

Suddenly, there was a sound in the closet that startled me! I sat straight up in bed. I listened intently -maybe I was dreaming-- after all what could be in my closet? I heard it again! It was a strange sound. I was frozen and couldn't move. I tried to say something, but no sound was coming out of my mouth. I was getting really scared! Why couldn't I say anything? I couldn't even get a squeak out.

Again I heard the sound. I knew that I had heard something that time. I tried to yell, again nothing, not one sound came out of my mouth! The sound in the closet became louder and louder. Suddenly I found myself crawling out of my bed. I didn't want to get out of my bed, but my body would not stop moving. I didn't have any control of my legs or arms! I thought about my father sleeping in his bed just upstairs. I tried to scream for him, "Dad! Dad!" I felt my mouth move, but I didn't hear my voice.

My fear was overtaking all my senses. After all my screaming, no sound had come out of my mouth. Why didn't I hear any sound? Then I realized that I wasn't awake. I was dreaming! I pleaded to myself, please wake up! I found my legs moving without my control. Step by step, I moved closer and closer to the closet. The air was very thick and time seemed to slow down. My body was moving step by step against my will.

Every step I took brought me closer and closer to my closet doors. I was being pulled by a power I could sense, but couldn't stop. Then all of sudden I stopped moving. I looked up and I was standing in front of the closet door. All I wanted to do was turn around and run back to bed. No matter what I did I couldn't get my legs to move away from the door. I stood frozen staring into the opening between the slats in the doors. I was no longer afraid, I was frozen inside of my body from terror.

I was standing in front of the door where I knew there was something waiting on the other side. Something so frighten that I never wanted to open that door! I knew what was lurking on the other side. I could feel its presence from the closet where it stood. I was pleading with myself. Wake up!

At that moment, I felt something reaching out to grab me. It was the presence of evil flowing like smoke filling a room. It poured through the opening in the slats of the door and engulfed my body. My skin started to crawl like it was trying to pull back. This was evil! Not imaginary evil, real evil. Its presence felt like the touch of rotting flesh against my skin. This was the kind of evil that made me want to run and hide. I knew there was no hiding from this. My skin felt like as if it was being seared by something far colder than ice.

Time stopped. I stood there frozen in terror as my skin turned ice cold. I felt the warmth leave my body. No, it wasn't the warmth leaving my body; it was the warmth leaving my soul. I was screaming inside my mind to run, please just let me run. Then, in that second, I saw a glimpse of what was standing inside the closet waiting for me. Through the slats, I could see eyes. Those eyes looked right through my body into my soul. The eyes were shaped like cat's eyes and there was a yellow fire in them. I stood as a petrified bird frozen in place with fear when it realizes that its claw was ready to strike. Again I pleaded with myself. Wake up, please let me wake up!

I looked down with horror at what was happening as I couldn't stop my arm from moving. I saw my hand reaching for the doorknob. I tried to stop my hand with every ounce of my will, but the movement did not slow down. Like a puppet, I was being forced to reach for the knob. I had no will of my own. All I felt was terror. The doorknob was in my hand. No! I screamed, yet no one heard me. It was too late! My hand was turning the knob and at that moment the closet door POPPED open!

Mercy and goodness were on my side at that moment! I awoke just as the door opened. I shot up in my bed; sweat was pouring down my face and arms. I trembled with fear, and not any ordinary fear. I shook from the fear that comes when you have a brush with real evil. It took me several minutes to gather myself. I jumped from my bed and ran to the light switch on the wall next to the bedroom door. My hand found the switch and I turned on the light. I stood for several more minutes, I did not dare move. Then, I slowly crept over to the closet door and peered between the slats.

I could see my hanging clothes. I reached for one of the doorknobs after looking cautiously from many different angles. Preparing to run, I opened one of the doors. The door being spring loaded busted open. It scared me to death!

Nothing was there but clothes. I decided it had all been a bad dream. No, not a bad dream it had been a terrible nightmare. After all the bad dreams that I had, this one scared me more than any I had before. This dream was not the worse to come. Several hours went by before I was able to settle down and to go back to sleep. I slept the rest of the night with the lights on.

The next morning I awoke tired and sleepy. By the time I got to the breakfast table I was running late for school. The day went by as usual. I had somewhat forgotten about the terrible nightmare when I arrived home from school. After all, I had bad dreams all my life. By nightfall I was more determined than ever to find the answers I was searching in my books! I studied twice as hard as I understood the urgency to know all there was about demonology. When I was finished reading I set all four books in a neat pile. I stacked each reference book on top of the other. I checked the closet before crawling into bed. I was so tired I fell asleep immediately.

All of a sudden I heard a sound. I sat straight up in the bed. I had heard that sound before. I told myself, you know that noise! Don't move and maybe it will go away. I was telling myself this as if it would help, but it was too late! I heard the sound again. It was coming from the closet.

I screamed, No, not again! I don't want to do this. Then I questioned myself. Is this a dream or am I awake? I decided that I was awake. I tried to call for my dad. I was screaming, "DAD!" As I screamed my lips moved yet my ears heard nothing. The sound was only in my head. Fear began to take over. This didn't make any sense. I screamed again, but this time I knew there wasn't any sound coming from my mouth.

This was a dream! And I knew that I could not wake up from it. Panic took over. I knew that I was locked into a nightmare. There was no way out for me. I thought to myself, if only I could get up. My body would not move. I tried to move my legs, my arms, any part of my body, but I couldn't. I cannot explain what it was like to be locked in your body and sitting there frozen in my bed. Then I heard the sound again.

New fear washed over me as I realized the reason I could not move was a direct result of what was in my closet. As my body began to move time slowed down. I could sense my legs moving without my control. I felt paralyzed. Now I was getting out of bed. I tried to will my legs from moving, yet I couldn't. Again I screamed but no sound came out. I was screaming and screaming in my mind when I just stopped. Suddenly I realized I was standing directly in front of my closet door.

The last place that I wanted to be. Why couldn't I walk over to my bedroom door? I did not want to stop here! I was moving my head for a better angle to see between the wooden slats in the door. If I could move my head, why couldn't I move my feet? I could not see anything through the opening in the slats. At that moment I could feel the presence in my closet. The hair stood up on the back of my neck. Every fiber of my being was screaming,

RUN, just run! Then horror struck as I saw my hand reaching out and grabbing the doorknob. I was thinking OK it's time to wake up! I watch as my hand pulled the door to my closet open.

There it stood! I was frozen in fear at the very sight of the beast. At that moment I knew it wasn't a beast, it was a demon. Its skin was covered with scales. The green scales covered most of the demons body except around the face and neck where the scales were light brown with touches of yellow splotches. It had a long ear on each side of its head that rose up to a sharp point that stopped about one-half inch above the top of its head. As it breathed, I could see under that skin covered with scales was a body with huge muscles. With each breath I could see them ripple like giant cables of steel. Its eyes were shaped like eyes of a cat watching its prey. The demon's eyes were yellow and they looked like they were on fire. It had huge nostrils, but it was breathing through its mouth. The teeth were large covered with foul greenish slime. Out of its mouth were two large fangs that were off-white from wear.

It let out a heavy breath and the stench hit me in the face. It was like smelling rotten flesh, death, and everything unclean that I could imagine. I felt that I had been engulfed in the foulness of its breath. I couldn't stand to breathe in the air. I stopped breathing through my nose. I gasped for air by opening my mouth and sucking in air. The stench was so bad it burned my throat. I coughed while trying to catch my breath. This made the beast laugh and its laughter sounded like scraping of barrels down a deep pit.

Its arm came up and I saw a claw where it should have been a hand and where there should have been fingernails, it had claws like an animal. It placed its claw on my shoulder and I wrenched with pain. The claw felt like red hot irons that had been pulled right out of the coals of a blacksmith furnace on my skin. I started to pull back from its grip, but I stopped. As soon as I started to pull away the beast locked its claws on my shoulder! I could feel them cutting through my flesh like sharp knives cutting warm butter. I knew it was too late to escape! It had me and I was helpless to escape.

There are times when you sense your luck has just run out. This was one of those times. I could feel the beast claws pressing deeper and deeper into my flesh. The more I pulled away, the more pain I felt in my shoulder.

Just then the demon spoke, "You are not very smart. If you pull back anymore I will take great pleasure in tearing your shoulder off. Yes, I could do that, you know. Tear your shoulder off."

The surprising part was its voice. This monster was speaking with a clear, calm deep voice. Its voice was so calming that it sounded like a doctor or teacher giving me instructions. I was stunned because its voice was not like its laugh. There was a certain tone that was pleasant and luring. I found myself finding comfort in its words as if I wanted it to say more to me. I must have stopped pulling because I felt its grip release slightly on my shoulder.

I asked, "What do you want with me?" Not the best of questions, but it was all I could get out of my mouth which seem to be working again.

It smiled and in doing so it showed those slimy green teeth again. "Oh, what I want with you is not the issue. No, I don't get what I want this time because I'm just the messenger. Yes, I would like to play with you for a while." My skin crawled at the thought. There was a coldness in what it said about playing with me. I know that I never want to know what playing meant to this demon. The demon tilted its head as if thinking, and as it stood there a smile came over its mouth. I was sure it was reading my mind by the look in its eyes. I would have fainted if the beast had not spoken again.

"What a shame that I don't get to play. NO, NO, I'm only here to give you a message tonight. I'm sure we will have time to play another night." It paused and smiled at that thought. That smile made my stomach retch as it seemed to take great pleasure in its thoughts of playing with me. I realized at that moment that this was not an ordinary demon, no it was far worse as it was very intelligent demon. Then its eyes focused again on me and said, "Yes the message, after all, that is why I'm here isn't it?" Again it tilted its head as if in thought and then said, "Oh yes, stop reading those books."

The demon let go of my shoulder and the next thing I knew I was sitting in the middle of my bed. Sweat was pouring down my face yet I was ice cold. My shoulder felt like it had been ripped open to the bone. I jumped out of my bed and ran over to the light switch. I was sure that when I turned on the light I would find my shoulder had been sliced to pieces.

I flip on the light and to my surprise there wasn't any blood or even a scratch on my shoulder. While I was very upset and my shoulder hurt, there wasn't a scratch anywhere. I was not as scared as the night before. Don't take this wrong, I was stilled scared, just not as scared as the night before. I checked out the closet and again there wasn't anything there. I went back to my bed and once again I left the light on. Needless to say, I didn't get much sleep for a second night.

After school and before I went to bed, I broke out my books on demonology. After all, the answers to all my troubles had to be in one of these books. Before I knew it was 10:30 PM. I had to get some sleep. School had been rough since I had not really slept in two nights. I crawled into bed, but I was smarter this night. I left my bedroom light on.

Sometime in the night I heard a noise in my closet. My heart missed a beat as fear washed over me. I sat up in bed thinking, did I really hear something?

Something did not look right, the bedroom was dark. What had happened to the light? Then it hit me. No, not again! I heard a sound for a second time. And it was definitely coming from my closet. I kept thinking to myself, almost as if I was talking to myself, something is not right. That when I realized that I was dreaming again. I could not wake up.

Why me, I thought? Please don't make me go through this nightmare again. But it was too late as I found myself walking to my closet door. I could see my hand reaching for the doorknob. I was helpless to stop this nightmare. All I could do was watch my actions replay all over again. I pleaded within to stop and wake up when I spotted movement through the planks in the doors.

Why is it that when I think there is something behind the door and no matter how scared I am, I have to open the door? My imagination was running wild as me hand reaches for the doorknob. I could not stop myself from opening that door. I knew what was waiting for me. And it was a Demon! Still, I could not stop my hand from opening that door. It was all a dream. A dream that I could not wake up from! I keep thinking. Please let me wake up! Too late, the door was opening!

The demon sprang on me as quick as a cat on a mouse. I felt the weight of the demon's body hit me and was helpless in protecting myself. As we hit the floor I was crushed by its weight. The hard mass of its body pinned me to the floor. The demon's sharp scales were rubbing against my skin. Wherever the scales touched my skin they dug into it like sandpaper. Every movement felt like the scales were rubbing off my skin. The blow had knocked the breath right out of me and I thought that I would pass out. It was wishful thinking, but I wasn't that lucky. I tried to suck in air, but my head was under the demon's head. All I could suck in was its breath. Smells have a way of bringing back memories, especially bad memories. The smell of rotten flesh, death, and evil brought back every memory of the night before. At that moment, I knew this really was pure evil.

Yes, this was a real demon. Not something in my nightmares, far worse. It was a real demon! This was a creature from the depths of hell. Fear does not even start to explain what I felt at that moment. There are not any real words that can describe how I was feeling at that realization. Unless you have been lying under a real demon, you cannot understand this terror. I was trying to regain some control before I went insane.

"Yes. Yessss, you are a stubborn little boy. Yes, I get to play with you now!" The demon said to me. In a very strange way, it was that voice that saved me from going mad! I had forgotten how alluring and calming the demons voice was. It spoke with somewhat of a lisp, yet it was so easy to listen to.

It's hard to explain, but at that moment I regained some courage and from out of my mouth I could hear myself saying, "You can't kill me, this is a dream!" I didn't even know I could think, and yet had I had spoken those words. I could feel the demon's anger boiling as it sucked air in its lungs.

"Yes, this is a dream!" The demon bellowed at me. "Yes, I can kill you, you are a foolish boy!" And then the demon just laid one claw on my leg and the pain shot through my whole body. I shook uncontrollably as my muscles went into spasms.

"You can hurt me and cause me physical pain, you can do that!" I screamed through the pain that spread over my body! I didn't really know where my words came can from at that point.

The demon just laughed at me. Even its laughter brought a wave of pain over me. "Yes, you are a stubborn and foolish little boy. Yes, I will enjoy playing with you. Yes, maybe we can play every night because I would like that, but my master said, I'm here to give you a message. Too bad I have to give you a message. Still I have to obey my master. His message is stop reading those books. Please don't! So I can come and play again with you!' There was a pleading in the demon's voice that almost made me want to do what it had asked. Despite all the fear and pain the demon's voice was so alluring that part of me was swayed.

Then I woke up sitting in my bed, wet with sweat and my leg throbbing as if it was broken. My skin felt like sandpaper had scrubbed me from head to toe and my light was still on in my bedroom as I realized again it was only a dream. I looked at my leg for bruises. There was none to be seen, but the pain was real. I could barely move my leg. I lay there for a long time; I was too scared to be sleep.

I made a decision the very next day that I had enough. I gathered up the books and gave them to my sister to return to the library. I sat in my chair at my desk before I went to bed and said out loud, "OK, I stopped reading those books, now leave me alone!" I got up and walked over to my bed. Soon after I crawled under the covers, I fell asleep. That night I had normal dreams of any sixteen year old boy.

CHAPTER 2
UNEXPECTED TRIP HOME

"I don't mean to imply that I'm afraid of death. I'm just not ready to go out on a date with him."- D Koontz

Eight years later. I was living by myself in a small two-bedroom house in the–country I had purchased. It was a white frame farmhouse with a large oak tree in the back yard. The house was old house with a back door that led through the kitchen and out into the back yard where the big old oak tree stood. The kitchen had been added to the back of the house along with a small utility room, years before.

From the kitchen you could access a second room that appeared to have been the original kitchen. The house did have a front door in the living room which I kept locked because I rarely used it. I used the back door as my main entrance and exit. I didn't own a key to the back door, so it was locked only from inside. Now looking back it's hard to believe that I lived in a house where I could not lock a back door. There was a small hallway off the living room leading to the bedrooms and bath.

I owned a Skating Rink in the small town of Gainesboro, Tennessee. Gainesboro was about eighteen miles from my house. I worked construction during the day and opened the skating rink on weekends. One weekend Pam and some of her friends drove do to my Skating Rink. While Pam was trying to make her way out on the skating floor, I offer to help her. I spent some time explaining the basis foot work of skating. That's how I met Pam who at that time lived in Red Boiling Springs, Tennessee. Before she left that night I asked her for a phone number. Week or so latter I had asked her out. That first date turned into a second and third date.

Shortly after we met and by our third date her family moved to a small farm at the edge of Kentucky just a few miles north of Lafayette, Tennessee. On Friday and Saturday nights Pam would get a ride to the rink. After closing, I would take her home in my 1974 Z28 Camaro. It was brown with a big black stripe that went down the hood and then down the trunk over the spoiler where Z28 was outlined in white with black lettering. The interior was cool with black leather. My Z28 had bucket seats, full instrumentation dash, and a flat steering wheel with leather padding. It had six-inch front and twelve-inch rears chrome rally wheels, air shocks, and a three hundred and fifty cubic inch motor with dual tailpipes.

It was one hot car with a built in eight track. The drive to take Pam home was a fifty-five mile trip from her house back to mine. That drive from her house to mine would also take me through several of the back roads in the middle of nowhere.

We would close the Skating Rink down at 10:30 PM, be out by 11:00 PM, and I would take her home. I am very much a creature of habit. So every night after I dropped Pam off I would head back home. I would stop at the market on the main drag in Lafayette. I always bought fried chicken, tater wedges, and a Mountain Dew to drink on the way home.

I was starving by that time from skating all night. I always stopped at that same little market due to timing. The market would be getting ready to close just about that time of night I pulled up. So they would give a good deal on the fried chicken that had not sold. Their chicken was deep-fried and so were the tater wedges. The market would drop the fried chicken and tater wedges into a paper box. I wasn't use to store bought deep fried chicken, and for a country boy like me, this was the best chicken I had ever had!

The chicken was all crunchy on the outside with juicy white meat on the inside. It would be little tough from lying under all those big red heat lamps all night. I loved it that way! It was

19

better to chew on as I drove down the road home in the middle of the night. I loved their potato wedges. And they were a real deal as what they did give me would be tossed. I would get all the skinny pieces that no one else wanted. They were breaded with a special batter and dropped in hot grease. By the time I picked up the tater wedges, they had been there for some time and were quite tough, just the way I liked them too. One man's throw-a-ways is another man's delight. This was prelude to a great drive home after a long night of skating.

Let me explain the roads I would take on the drive home. From Lafayette I would head east on Highway #52 to Red Boiling Springs, southeast on Highway #151 to North Springs, east on Highway #56 to Whitleyville, then stay on Highway #56 through Gainesboro, continuing on Highway #56 South to Old Gainesboro Road and then to my house. Most of these roads are very hilly with lots of curves. This was not a fast drive home as it takes time to winding through the curves and speeding was not wise.

Driving the back roads of this area of Tennessee there are many small towns. Many of those towns are no longer there except for the old town sign. Some of those small towns are no more than just a wide place in the road. And for a few there's only a road signs now proclaiming that they once existed. There are two sharp curves on Highway #56 just outside of Whitleyville. This section of Highway #56 the road is very crooked except for two long straight sections of the road just before you entered each of the two pin curves. (Pin Curve is a country saying for a curve that curves back about three hundred and thirty degrees, just like a hair pin.) The first pin curve was not as sharp as the second one. I used the first pin curve as a road marker to slow down on the next straight section of road or I wouldn't have a chance at making the second curve. The second curves' road banked sharp which would let the car drift high. If you drifted too high, you would end up in the guardrail, or worse, over the guard rail.

On one particular Saturday night drive home I was listening to the radio and thinking it was a shame that all my chicken was gone. I just reached into the paper box digging around to make sure there wasn't one last piece of chicken hiding there. When I looked up, I was staring at the guardrail of the second pin curve. I thought, to myself; this can't be right. I haven't hit the first curve! I realized that it was too late to worry about that as I grabbed the steering wheel with both hands and slammed on the brakes.

Everything went into slow motion. I felt the car drifting sideways and I knew that I was going to hit the guardrail at any second. Oh no, this is the second pin curve! I keep saying to myself. I couldn't believe that I was in the second pin curve. I still could not remember going through the first pin curve. Everything was wrong! I glanced down at my dash to see how fast I was going. The speedometer said seventy miles per hour and dropping fast. I remember thinking. This is way too fast!

I knew I would never make it. I looked out my windshield to gage how much time I had before I hit the guardrail. I could see my headlights shining over the side of the curve and out into the air. I was drifting high but still too fast for the curve. I looked back down at my dash and my speed was down to fifty miles per hour and still dropping. I thought; still too fast for this curve. And I'm too high! I'll never make it.

Just as I looked back at the road, my headlights went out and there was total darkness. As I stared out of my car's windshield, I reached for the light switch on the dash with my left hand. I started thinking it was time to brace myself for impact. Time was slowing down as I should have hit the guardrail by now. I said to myself, "Where is that switch?" My hand had not found the light switch; I looked down at the dash to find it. Out loud, I said, "What's going on?" I couldn't see the dash lights. All was dark in the car.

I thought I would feel the crush of the guardrail against the side of my car any second. Then I noticed the radio had gone silent. I reached out into the darkness searching for the dash to find the light switch, but the dash wasn't there. I couldn't believe the dash was gone! I leaned forward and felt with my left hand. I had my arm extended as far as possible and still I couldn't feel anything. I took my left hand and waved it all around in front of me, nothing. I was thinking. This can't be right. Where is the dash, the windshield, the door? They were all gone! I still had hold of the steering wheel in my right hand. So I leaned back in my seat and grabbed the steering wheel with my left hand.

I fought for several seconds as I was trying to keep from panicking. The only thing keeping me from going over the edge with fear was the steering wheel. I gripped it with both hands still believing that I would feel the impact any second. Thoughts raced through my mind, maybe I have been thrown out of the car. That would explain what was happening. Yet it didn't make any sense. I hadn't felt the impact of my car hitting the guardrail. Had I been thrown out of the car and I took the steering wheel with me? But why was I sitting in the middle of a field?

No. There wasn't a crash and I was still sitting in the bucket seat of my 1974 Camaro. I could feel the seat under me. Within seconds I felt the steering wheel melt in my hands. The next second I could feel the soft leather covering in my hands. A second later it turned into sand and was gone. I panicked! What was going on? I reached as far as I could with both hands in front of me and side to side. Nothing! No lights, no dash, no windshield, no radio, no steering wheel, nothing. Wait, my bucket seat. Yes, I was still sitting in my seat. I reached down and I could feel the sides of my seat. I pulled up on the sides as this was the only solid thing left to hold on to! At that moment I lost consciousness.

The next thing I recall I was sitting up in darkness. I was scared to death. My legs straight out, not bent like they were when I was sitting in my bucket seat. It was jet black and I couldn't see anything. I felt around me with my hands in the darkness to figure out what I was sitting on. I felt cloth beneath me; a large area of cloth. It felt familiar. In that moment I realized that I was sitting in bed. A small amount of light was pouring through the windows. The windows in a bedroom. My eyes began to adjust to the light in the room. I knew where I was. I was in my bed, at my house.

I jumped up out of bed and turned on the light. There at the foot of my bed were my clothes. I was shocked because they had been neatly folded; pants on the bottom, then my shirt, and my socks were neatly folded on top. My keys, wallet, and change were lying next to my socks on my shirt. Just under the side of my bed were my shoes, tucked under the edge of the bed. My clothes looked just like a scenic out of a movie, not the way you throw your throw off your clothes in the real world. I ran through the house to the kitchen door and looked out to see if my car was there. I started out the backdoor and almost broke my arm. The door was locked. I turned the kitchen light on in order to unlock the door.

I opened my backdoor and ran out barefooted and in my underwear. I checked my car and it was fine. The hood was still warm from the engine. My car was sitting where I always parked it. I walked back into the house. I didn't lock my back door on the way to my bedroom. I couldn't figure out how I had gotten home. I could not have been driving in my sleep. How could I get from that pin curve to my bedroom? It was a long drive from that pin curve on Highway 356 down to Gainesboro. It wouldn't be for several years that I found out what really happened.

Chapter 3
Un-Welcome Visitor

"No, thank you. We don›t want any more visitors, well-wishers, or distant relations."~ Lord of the Rings

Pam and I dated for a short while and in the spur of the moment ran off one Saturday and got married. Pam had live at the edge of Kentucky some fifty miles away and I felt it was too far to keep driving! In my mind it was breakup or get married. We got married and we fought, a lot. We really didn't know each other and had we dated longer we probably wouldn't have married. Pam came from a large family, and though she lived in the country, she had brothers and sisters to visit with during the day. Married to me, she was faced with living in a house where she was alone all day. Often, she would walk over to a large graveyard across the road in a field some distance from our house. Both Pam and I believe that was where our unwelcomed visitor came from. The graveyard.

Pam missed having someone around to talk to. One day while Pam was sitting in the graveyard crying she asked out loud how much she needed a friend. She should have been more careful where she asked for a friend! That night, after we had gone to bed, I sensed a presence in our house. I did not say anything to Pam as I did not want to scare her. It wasn't an evil present, but I did sense a spirit. As the days went by, little things began to happen.

One evening at supper Pam told me while she was washing out the bathtub, she thought I had sneaked home to surprise her. She began telling me what happened. She said, "I was bent over the tub running water when I felt drops of water hit my back. I thought you had thrown some water on me as a trick! I jumped up mad and happy to see you come home early. Yet when I turned around, you weren't there! I thought maybe you were hiding, so I called for you. "Wayne, that wasn't funny, throwing water on me!" But you never answered. First, I got mad. It wasn't funny anymore. Then I started to get scared. The house was quiet. I started walking through the house to find you. You weren't there. Then I really got scared when I realized that you weren't in the house.

I didn't know what to say as I explained, "Pam, I was at work all day". I told her. "Maybe you just splashed yourself?" I wasn't sure what happened, but I had an uneasy feeling about what she had just said.

"No!" she said with fear in her voice. "Someone threw water on me! I could feel them standing behind me, but when I turned around, no one was there. I was sure it was you pulling a joke on me. My dress was soak and wet."

I didn't know what to say and I didn't want her to be scared yet I had an idea what might have happened. And I didn't dare say another word.

Several days passed. It was Saturday night and Pam and I had just come home after closing the Skating Rink. We were starving. Pam started cooking hamburgers while I ran to the bathroom. Just as I took a seat on the john there came a bang on the bathroom door. BANG, BANG, BANG!

"All right, I'll be out in just a minute!" I said in an angry tone of voice. Nothing is worse than having only one bathroom in the house. Again, BANG, BANG, BANG! That time she almost busted the wood on the door. I thought, she went too far, "Look, give me a minute!" I shouted at her. As soon as I finished, I marched out of the bathroom to ask why she couldn't wait for me to finish. And why she kept banging on the door. I marched straight to the kitchen where Pam stood over the stove and asked, "Couldn't you wait until I was done?"

Wayne Louis

"What are you talking about?" Pam asked as she flipped one of the burgers in the skillet.

"I'm talking about you beating on the bathroom door!" She looked at me puzzled.

"What are you talking about? I've been standing here cooking supper!" She said with a confused look on her face.

I realized that it wasn't her who knocked on the bathroom door. I let it drop because I was scared and the last thing I wanted was for Pam to be upset and scared as well.

A few days passed and all was fine. Nothing unusual happened. The peace did not last very long. A day or two later I pulled into the driveway, and noticed Pam sitting out in the front yard. As I got out of the car she came running up to me and threw her arms around me.

"Thank goodness you are home!" She said with tears in her eyes. "What's wrong?" I asked.

She started to cry, "I wasn't feeling well after lunch so I decided to lie down and take a nap. I was just about to doze off when the door to the bedroom slammed shut! It scared me to death! I jumped out of bed and ran to the door and opened it. I got chills as it felt like someone was standing there next to me. But there wasn't anyone in the house but me. I ran outside and I've been too scared to go back in the house."

I did my best to calm her down. I told Pam that I would check out the house. I walked in and there wasn't anybody in the house. I came back out and reassured her that it was the wind that had blown the door shut. I hated to lie as I knew it wasn't the wind.

The next day when I came home from work, Pam told me that she was walking out of the bathroom when she felt someone touch her so I asked her to explain.

'Well, I was stepping out of the bathroom into the hall when I felt a hand on my shoulder. It scared me! I turned to see if someone was behind me, but the hallway was empty. There was a chill in the air and I felt goose bumps all over. What's going on?' she asked.

There was no use in lying as I had felt the un-welcomed visitor in the house ever since the banging on the bathroom door. "I believe that we have a visitor in the house."

"What do you mean a visitor in the house?" she asked. I knew that she already knew what I was talking about.

"You told me a few days ago, you had been sitting by the graveyard crying. I believe that you said something about needing a friend. Well, it would appear that you now have one. I'm afraid it's not the kind of friend you wanted. We have to be careful what we ask for."

"What are saying? We have a ghost in our house and it's my fault?" She was both angry and frightened.

"Look, I didn't want to say anything, but I have felt it many times. I can't explain it, but I can sense spirits." I did not feel like telling her what had happened to me all these years in my dreams. I have been able to sense a spirits presences for a long time. I avoided having anything to do with the spiritual world since I had an encounter with a demon in the closet as a teenager.

Pam taking her anger out on me said, "So if you are so smart, how do we get rid of it?"

I said, "I could sense spirits NOT get rid of them!"

"Well, I guess you're not as smart as you think you are!" She said as she stomped off.

The activity continued from our un-welcomed guest for several weeks. Doors slamming shut, banging on doors, or feelings like someone was touching you only to find no one there became common occurrences in our home. One day I decided I had enough! We had an old pool table in the living room. *Awkward transition.* We didn't have living room furniture so I bought an old pool table for fifty dollars. It had a bed made of thin plywood instead of a slate, that it why I got it for fifty dollars. I was standing by the pool table when I said out loud, "I have had it with you! I want you out of our house! Come on, show yourself. I'm not afraid, here I am!" The room turned ice cold. "Good trick, but it still doesn't scare me! Get out of my house!" I stood there waiting for something to happen. Nothing! So I started to walk out of the room when I heard a loud "crack!" The sound was like a "break" that happens at the beginning of a pool game. It's that loud crack as the queue ball strikes the other balls. Then, I could hear the balls rolling over the table and dropping into the pockets. The thing is, I had cleaned off the table and placed all the balls in the pockets. I turned and looked at the pool table and, of course, there weren't any balls on the table, so I turned again walked out of the room.

That night everything came to a head. Pam and I had a hard time falling to sleep. We could feel the spirit in the house. Its presence was so strong that, not only could I feel it, but so could Pam.

Finally, we drifted off to sleep. I started to dream that a spirit was standing at our bedroom door. I don't remember what it looked like, as it really didn't have a physical body, even in my dream, it was just there. I said, "You are not welcomed in our house anymore, get out!" The spirit answered "No, you didn't invite me, she did, and I like it here!"

I jumped out of bed and ran for the door. When I got to the door, I grabbed the spirit and we began to fight. While it was only a dream, it seemed all too real. We had locked each other in a grip around our shoulders. Still the spirit did not have a physical body, but in some ways I could feel a solid body. I could feel it, touch it, and even grab hold of it. I could tell that this seemed to surprise the spirit that I could physically hold on to it. In our struggle, we hit the dresser in the bedroom and sent it crashing to the floor. Then we fell to the floor and the spirit was under me. I managed to get my feet under me and I grabbed it by the shoulders and I heaved with all my might! I lifted both of us off the floor and threw the spirit through the bedroom door with one quick motion saying "I said get out of my house, and I meant it!" The spirit had hit the hall wall and bounced off the wall to the floor. I did not wait for the spirit to get up. I pounced on it grabbing it again, throwing it through the hall into the living room. There it crashed into the pool table. I had thrown it with such force that the impact knocked the pool table over. It crashed on its side and the balls were rolling all over the room. I had lost the advantage of surprise; the spirit now knew that I could fight it on a physical realm. It jumped up and attacked. It launched itself at me, knocking me back into the hall. We both knew that this was more of a fight than either had expected. Only one of us would win and there would be no stopping until there was a victor.

I couldn't stop now, I jumped to my feet grabbed the spirit as I headed for the back door. I was pushing and pulling the spirit all the way. This was more than a physical battle of who was the strongest; it was also a battle of wills. Whoever had the strongest will win this battle. Somewhere along the way, I realized that I did have the inner power to win this battle.

I could draw on some type of endless inner power that would help me in this fight. Just knowing this gave me the will to win over this spirit. I realized the spirit was starting to understand that I was stronger that it thought possible for a mortal. I could sense a bit of fear in the spirit as it realized it might not come out as the victor. At the back door, the spirit made its final stand. As I started to push and shove the spirit against the back door it started to give away under the force. I could see the wood breaking, when at last the door gave way. The spirit grabbed at the door jams in one last fight to stay in the house. I found the power deep within me to make one last push. Then I threw the spirit out of our house. I could see it laying on the pieces of broken wood in my backyard. I said, "You are not welcome here anymore! If you come back I will throw you out again! Be gone and do not return!" I turned and walked back to the bedroom and slid back into my warm bed.

The next morning I woke to find that our dresser was still standing, not broken into pieces or lying sprawled all over the bedroom floor. What a relief, but as I sat up I found that I was very sore. While there were no bruises, there were sore spots where I had hit against the walls and floors during the fight. Thank goodness the backdoor wasn't torn off its hinges and lying in the backyard. As for the un-welcomed visitor, it never came back to our house. After a couple of days, I told Pam that I believed that the spirit was gone. She did not have any more pranks pulled on her after that night. I did not tell her what had happened in my dream; after all she wouldn't have believed me. I did give Pam very firm instructions, "Never go over to the graveyard again."

CHAPTER 4
TRADING A SOUL FOR A SOUL

"Be patient my soul thou hath suffered worse than this"
- Thomas Holcroft

Times got tough and I joined the Army. The economy had taken a turn for the worse and work was not to be found. I was living in a small town on the outskirts of Denver, Colorado. I was completing my training to be a Calibration Specialist for the United States Army. My rank wasn't high enough for on-base housing and the Calibration School was on an Air Force Base. The Air Force was not accommodating to Army students so we felt no love. Pam and I lived in a small apartment of base. And by this time, we had a son, Michael.

Our apartment was in a brick building three-stories high with four apartments on each level. The front of the building had a set of steps that lead to a big glass door that entered into the foyer at the second level. There was a lock on the door and visitors had to buzz someone to let them in. Our apartment was on the second level and to the left of the entrance. We had a one bedroom apartment, which was all we could afford. Often I worked part-time jobs to make ends meet. The living area and kitchen was one big room with a small bathroom and a bedroom with a big walk-in closet. Pam and I turned the walk-in closet to a small play area for our son, Michael.

We had our bed and a small child bed for Michael in the bedroom. His bed was very low to the floor and was a bit too short for a grownup to lay on. He was starting to walk and could get into his bed all by himself. Often he would get tired and crawl into bed for a nap.

Money was tight, but we made it. I had three months left in school when life changed after the arrival of a new tenant in our apartment building. *Transition sentence needed here as it sound like glen is the new tenant* Glen was in the apartment on the third floor directly above us. He was in the Army and had gone to school to be a nurse. I thought it odd, a man going to school to be a nurse. But that just shows how times have changed. Glen finished his schooling and was reassigned, so his apartment was available for rent.

A Staff Sergeant in the Air Force rented the apartment. His name was Mr. Nelson. I noticed the first time that I met him that he was rather strange. He was friendly and a little odd. He took an interest in Michael from the start. He would talk to Pam every chance he could and ask questions about Michael. He told us more about his life than we wanted to know.

He told us he had been married and now divorced for several years. He had two teenage daughters coming to spend two weeks with him. He had been stationed in the Philippines for the last two years and had not seen his daughters; he was only able to write to them. The day they arrived, he stopped by to introduce them to us.

A couple of days later I passed Mr. Nelson and his daughters in the hall. The girls gave me a look that was haunting, like they were begging for me to rescue them. The look bothered me as I felt like I had walked off knowing that something wasn't right. Mr. Nelson's daughters only stayed for a couple more days and they left to go back home. He told us that he was upset at his daughters! They had insisted he change their plane ticket and let them go home.

After the abrupt departure of his daughters, things started to get weird. Mr. Nelson started drinking, a lot! Often he came down to our apartment at night drunk. He started talking about getting into things that he couldn't get out of. Most of the time, Mr. Nelson rambled on and on about things that had happened to him in the Philippines. What he rambled about really never made any sense. We didn't try to understand his rambling. Then one night he told us that he was involved in some type of devil worshiping.

A couple of nights after that, we had just sat down to watch TV when there was a knock at the door. Pam went to the door and as she looked through the peephole she said, "Wayne, its Mr. Nelson. I'm not answering it, you get it."

"Why me?" I asked as I didn't want to talk to him and I sure did not want to let him in.

"Wayne, I need your help!" Mr. Nelson was saying from outside of the door. He must have heard us, so I opened the door. "Quick, you've got to come upstairs with me." There was panic in his voice, so up the stairs we went. I could not think of what could have happened to upset him so bad. His apartment door was wide open and in he went. I followed him right in without thinking!

"Come over here!" He said as he pointed to a spot by one of his stereo speakers. "Listen, there are voices coming out of my speakers."

"Of course, if you had your stereo on!" I said less than amused about being dragged up to his apartment to find out that his stereo speaker had voices coming out of it!

His expression quickly turned to anger. "The stereo wasn't on. The voices were not human; they were demons talking to me!"

"What did they say?" I asked, thinking that Mr. Nelson had been drinking a little too much and now I was in his apartment listening to him raging about demons.

"Put your ear next to the stereo speaker and listen, can hear them?" He said as he pointed to one of the speakers with the foam cover removed from the speaker box.

In an attempt to calm him down, I lowered my head and stuck my ear next to the speaker and listened. "All I hear is static, you don't have it on a station." I was ready to go.

"No, no they were talking to me." He said in panic mode. "I'm running out of time! You see I've made a deal and now they want me to pay!"

"How much money are you in for?" Was the first thing out of my mouth.

Again I had upset him! "No, it is not about money, they don't want money!" He was getting agitated with me and then he said, "They want my soul!"

That was it, Mr. Nelson this was getting too crazy for me. I didn't want any part of Mr. Nelson at this point so I headed for the door. I was leaving, I turned to Mr. Nelson and said, "I can't help you!"

Before I could get out the door he said, "You are wrong; you can help me with this, I can sense it. You could fight for me!"

This stopped me right in my tracks. "Wait one minute! I'm not getting involved in your mess. The last thing I'm going to do is fight for you!" I stormed out of the apartment. I was not sure what kind of mess Mr. Nelson had gotten himself into, but I was not going to get dragged in to it!

We did not see Mr. Nelson for a couple of weeks. One day while I was gone, Pam said that Mr. Nelson had stopped by the apartment. "What did he want this time?" I asked because I did not trust him.

"It was really odd," she said as she started to tell me what had happened. "Mr. Nelson said that he was balancing his check book so he could write checks to pay his bills. He said that after he writes his checks for his rent and all of his other bills, his remaining balance in his checking account was $666.00. He said that was a sign."

"What kind of sign?" I asked.

"He wasn't sure, but he said he couldn't leave his check book with that balance. He wrote a check for $100.00, tore it out of his checkbook and handed it to me. He said, "Why not buy Michael a new toy or something!"

"You didn't take it. did you?" I asked. I did not trust Mr. Nelson.

"Well, Mr. Nelson was so insistent that I take it. Besides we were out of milk. And you don't get paid until the end of the month and that is still a week away." Pam justified.

"So, you have spent the check?" I wasn't really angry, I felt bad that we were low on money. I had quit my part time job since I was in the last block of calibration training. Studying was absorbing more of time. I would be receiving a new assignment and we would be moving in a couple of weeks. I had a bad feeling about taking that check. Back then, one hundred dollars was equivalent to a thousand dollars today. In the Army with PFC pay it was not always easy to make ends meet. We lived right on the edge financially and often, we did without food to make ends meet.

"I'm sorry; I shouldn't have taken the check! Please don't get upset." Pam said pleading with me. After all, these were hard times for her too! "Look", she was holding a stuffed bear. "I bought Michael a new toy with part of the money."

I told her it would be OK and that I wasn't upset about the check. I said, "Well, I'm glad that someone has money to give away, even if it is Mr. Nelson."

A week later, it was Sunday night, and I remember it like yesterday. We had finished supper and Pam was cleaning up the kitchen. I was sitting down to watch my favorite show, Battlestar Galactica. I had put Michael in his bed for the night, gave him a kiss and pulled the door to the bedroom slightly closed. I liked the ability to hear him if he didn't go to sleep right away.

My television show had been on for about ten minutes when there was a blood-curdling scream coming from the bedroom. I jumped over the coffee table and ran into the bedroom where Michael was sitting in his bed. When he saw me he jumped from the side of his bed and latched onto my side. He was holding onto me like a cat and I could feel his tiny hands gripping like hands of steel. I couldn't have torn him off if I wanted to.

"Bite daddy, bite!" He was screaming as he pointed under the bed and again said, "Bite daddy, bite!" Michael was barely talking, so for him to put two words together was amazing. I told him it was all right and by that time Pam had made her way to the bedroom door and turned on the light.

"What in the world scared him?" she was asking.

"I'm not sure. He keeps saying, "Bite daddy, bite"' and then point under the bed. I managed to get Michael to let go of me and I handed him to Pam. I got down on the floor and was careful as I looked under the bed. This was not one of my favorite things to do. Nothing was there. I said, "Look Michael, there isn't anything under the bed!" It was no use he was sure that something was under his bed. I lifted his bed and show him nothing was there. That night he wouldn't lie in his bed. He slept with us. For the next couple of days, he wouldn't go into the bedroom and play without one of us in the room with him.

Pam asked me many times what I thought happened and I told her he had a bad dream, but I didn't really believe it. It was easier to pretend that it was a bad dream. We avoided Mr. Nelson for the next couple of days as we felt sure this had something to do with him.

During this time, there was one rather humorous thing that did happen after the disturbance in the bedroom with Michael. There were two young men who showed up at the apartment building. They were Seven Day Advent youths making their way out in the land. No one would let them in except for good old

Mr. Nelson. I watched as Mr. Nelson led them up the stairs and into his apartment as I was cleaning the hall floor. After about ten minutes I heard feet running down the stairs. I looked to see what all the commotion was about. The two young men were running down the stairs like the devil himself was after them. They about broke the front door down trying to get out of the building. I heard Mr. Nelson yelling from the top of the steps, "Don't leave me like this, I need your help!" They never slowed down on their way out. His pleads were only encouragement to run faster. They never stopped at our apartment building after that day. I did see them pass the apartment building as they travel down the sidewalk many times, they always picked up their stride as they passed our building.

Two weeks later, in the middle of the night, there was a knock at our door. I could hear the knocking, but I couldn't wake up. I heard the knocking again and managed to sit up in bed as something wasn't right. I could see, but the room was dark. Pam was sleeping and the knocking had not awakened her. I couldn't understand how she could sleep through the loud knocking. Michael was still asleep in his bed next to ours. I started to walk to the front door, but things just didn't feel right. All of a sudden the hair on the back of my neck began to tingle!

I knew something was at the door and I didn't want to let it in! I had felt that feeling before, it been a long time ago. I knew what was standing on the other side of the door. Should I wake Pam or let her sleep? Again a loud knock at the door but this time it was a louder. I had to open it! I reached for the doorknob and my skin started to crawl. I don't know why, but I opened the door.

Standing in the hall of our apartment, was a demon. It was somewhat human in form, but it was covered with scales. The scales were dark green with lighter colored scales on its chest and face. Muscles rippled like tight springs under the scales. It had powerful claws with long dirty nails on both its hands and feet. The top parts of its arms were dark green that faded into a light yellow-green on the inside of its arms and ran up to its armpits. Its arms were like a large tree trunk that extended from its body. Its arms were rippled with muscles under the skin of scales. Its face had a high ridge of bones that made up its eyebrow with scales covering its entire face. Its nose was flat like that of an ape. And it did have lips covered with small light green scales that opened to reveal long yellow teeth. It had two large fangs that protruded from the top section of its teeth. The eyes were red as fire where they should have been white. The cornea of its eyes had very distinct slits and they were yellow like the eyes of a cat. Then, I heard its voice. Which was deep as and loud, yet surprising clear? It spoke with the assurance of power and authority.

"I'm here for the trade!" it said in a loud voice that should have awakened the whole apartment building.

"What trade?" I replied, just like you would ask a traveling salesman who was standing at my door.

"I'm here for the child that was traded." There was more than a tinge of annoyance in its voice. I could tell that the demon wasn't used to being questioned.

"There's no trade here, you must have the wrong door!" I, too, was showing my annoyance by the way I gave my answers to him. I was standing my ground.

"I don't have time to waste, let me have the boy child!" Its voice had changed from annoyance to anger since I would not step out of its way.

"Maybe you didn't hear me, there is no trade here!" I was thinking, "Where is Pam and why hadn't she gotten out of bed?" I needed her for support as I could see that things were going to get out of hand real soon. I knew this was a demon as I had been faced with this before. I clearly remember what happen the last time I been in this very spot and I wasn't sure I could keep this demon from taking Michael.

"Enough of this, out of my way!" as it reached for me with one of its claws.

I moved faster than I could believe was possible. I felt my body hit the demon's body and the scales felt like hitting sharp metal. Its body was hard as steel. It was almost like hitting a brick wall that moved. My move took the demon by surprise, which was my only good moment during this encounter. It was simple; the demon was used to its victims cringing with fear, not attacking. My attack only took the demon by surprise for a second, and then it moved with the speed of a cat. I felt its body roll as we fell to the floor and when we hit, I was on bottom.

"You are quite surprising for a mortal," it hissed at me. "I understand now why they sent me! Yes, you're not all you seem."

I did not let go of my grip, even though I felt the demon was three times more powerful than I was. I couldn't even lift its weight off of me. I struggled to flip it off. "I'm not letting you have my son!"

This made the demon laugh, "You think that you can stop me? I could kill you right now if I so choose to." The demon leaned close to my face and I could feel its hot breath on my face. Like a wind from a fiery pit, it scorched the side of my face. Its breath was foul smelling, like rotting meat.

"Kill me if you can, but I won't let you have my son!" I yelled back. There was something in me that said I would not lose this battle. I gathered all my strength and pushed the demon off of me. I grasped the doorknob and pulled it shut. Of course that meant that I had just closed the door with both of us standing in the hall. I should have closed the door after I jumped through first. It wasn't one of my smarter moves. It was too late; I had slammed the door closed. The demon let out a roar, and then it was on me again. It knocked me across the hall like a cat batting a mouse. I felt my body hit the wall and bounced off like a rag doll. I couldn't lose this fight. Somehow I picked myself up and lunged at the demon as it was turning the doorknob with its claw. We went flying down the hall and landed on the floor, but this time I was on top.

"You don't listen very well! I said you cannot have my son!" But just like before, the demon was quicker and stronger. I found myself sailing across the hall again.

"I like playing with you, even though I don't have time to play this night. It's been a very long time since I have met someone who tries to put up a fight." It laughed as I could see a smile on its face. The Demon liked throwing me around the hall like a rag doll. I realized that it had the door open and was about to enter our apartment. I made a swipe for its leg with one hand as I jump trying to knock it off balance. I was holding its leg with all the strength I had left in me. My weight on the leg was just enough to throw it balance off. It hit the door jam and bounced back into the hall. I jumped back on top of its body and held on. Just then I saw the first rays of sunlight shooting through the window. The demon was furious; it threw me off and stood up.

"You have won this night, but it is not over!" With that the demon was gone.

Moments later I woke to the alarm clock ringing. I jumped out of bed. It scared me to death! I was wet with sweat as I reached over and turned the alarm off. Pam was attempting to wake up. I stood up and was so tired I could barely move. Every muscle felt like it had been beaten with a baseball bat. I was taking a shower, getting ready for work and I couldn't sort out what had happened last night. Was it a dream? Was it real? I didn't mention a word of this to Pam. Things were getting weird. I received my orders and in two weeks we would be gone. I was thinking why say anything now?

Two days later, on a Saturday morning, we were packing the apartment for our move. Pam stopped what she was doing and said, "I know you are going to think I'm crazy, but I have to tell you this. Two nights ago I had this terrible dream! I dreamed that something was knocking at our door. I just laid there when you went to answer the door because I couldn't move. I could see you even though I wasn't there. When you opened the door there was a monster standing there. It had come for Michael! Something about a trade, but you wouldn't let it in. Then you started fighting with the monster as I tried to get up to help you, but I couldn't move. It was the scariest dream I have ever had! I tried to get up out of the bed and check on Michael. I couldn't move in the bed, it was like I was frozen. I felt so bad that I couldn't come to help you or even check on Michael. I wasn't going to say anything, but I have to ask? Was it real or just a dream?"

"I'm not sure! I believe it was a dream. Now that you told me this, I'm just not sure what it was. I had the same dream. And even though I don't have any bruises, I'm so sore that I can still barely move from the fight." We both knew that it was Mr. Nelson. He had tried to make some type of trade. We didn't say much more about the dream because some things are better left alone. We were glad to be moving in just a few days. We also thought it was best to throw the stuffed bear away. After all, it had been bought with the money Mr. Nelson gave us.

CHAPTER 5
SAYING GOODBYE TO MR. NELSON

"Darkness cannot drive out darkness: only light can do that"
–Martin Luther King

The next several days went by without any trouble as we got ready to move. We stayed away from Mr. Nelson and avoided him by ducking into our apartment or driving around the block until he was gone. We did not answer the door if he came down and knocked.

On the last day as we were leaving, we had the U-Haul loaded and were ready to go when Mr. Nelson met me in the hall.

"I see that you are all ready to go." He asked, "Could you stop in before you leave; I would like to say goodbye." I couldn't say no because he seemed like a broken man. It's hard to walk way for a person in need. I always feel obligated to help someone and at that point Mr. Nelson needed a friend. Despite all he had done, I agreed to stop by and say goodbye.

I must have lost all my wit about me. I had no idea just how far Mr. Nelson was willing to go to save himself, but I was about to find out. Why did I agree to stop in to say goodbye to him? I had the car packed and ready to go. I left Pam and Michael sitting in the car waiting on me. I made one last trip up the stairs to Mr. Nelson's apartment and I knocked on his door.

Mr. Nelson opened the door and with a big smile said, "Come in, come in Wayne! Where are Pam and Michael?" Mr. Nelson was so glad to see me. He was smiling for ear to ear.

"They're in the car; packed and ready to go. I can only stay a second. You asked me to come by and say goodbye, so this is it!" I reached for the doorknob when he said, "Wait, I know that things got a little out of hand, but it wasn't my fault!" He pleaded. "I had got into some trouble, and it's really a long story, but you could help me!" He had the look of a drowning person who was praying I would throw him a life preserver. "Wayne, you are special. You could fight for me. You could win my soul back! I know you could!" He wasn't just asking, he was pleading. Have you ever seen an animal trapped and suddenly thinks it has found a way out! This was Mr. Nelson.

"I'm not sure what kind of trouble you are in, but I can't fight for you!" I was not about to go down any path with Mr. Nelson. I knew that I couldn't trust him!

"What, you wouldn't help a friend?" As he began to anger the room turned to ice. Goose bumps from the chill broke out on my arms. Mr. Nelson's face changed and as the anger in him grew, it was gone as he smiled.

"Wayne, you are special. You have great powers that you don't even know about!" The words were coming out of Mr. Nelson's mouth, but it wasn't his voice. The voice tones and the way he talked sounded like an old southern preacher. As I listened to Mr. Nelson, the memory of apple pie came to mind and I all but forgot where I was at.

"Wayne, my child, my master loves you! He is willing to do anything to help you! My master takes care of his own. All he wants in return is for you to love and worship him." He sounded like a good old southern preacher. His words flowed with long drawn out breaths. I could see myself sitting back in a rocking chair as all my troubles started to melt away as I listened to his voice.

Suddenly I thought, his master! Who was his master? Then I asked, "Are you talking about God?"

"Yes my Lord, he is a God!" Mr. Nelson was smiling as the words came out of his mouth.

"You didn't answer my question. Who is your master?" I noticed that the room had grown colder and I could see my breath as I was talking, and this wasn't a dream! I was standing in the room talking to Mr. Nelson or what used to be Mr. Nelson at 10:00 AM.

"My master has many names, but he likes to be called Lord as any God." Once again Mr. Nelson gave me that sweet smile.

"So we are talking about God, the God of the heavens?" I wanted to make sure we were on the same page.

"Oh, that God? No, no, no! After all, what has he ever done for you? My master and lord, has many names! You know he once was an archangel, but now he rules over this world. He has dominion over this land." Once again he smiled with that look of someone offering you a piece of hot apple pie. Yet I could feel the jaws of the trap starting to close! And I was the prey.

"We are not talking about the same God. If I remember, who you are talking about was an archangel once, but that was before he was cast down. Besides, I will stick with my God, holy of the holies!" This was all I needed to say.

Anger boiled in Mr. Nelson's face for a second, but he quickly regained his composure. "God, your God? What has he ever done for you? When you needed money, did he give you money? When you were hungry, did he give you food? When you were sick did he comfort you? What has he ever really done for you?" He smiled with the face of a true friend. "My master loves his own and will help them! All you have to do is love him back. Wayne, what do you want out of life? Rank in the army? You can have as many stripes as you want! If you want out of the army he can make that happen. Just ask him! I know money, you need money! How much? All you have to do is ask."

Mr. Nelson stood there for a second and I wasn't sure what he would do or say next.

"Wayne, this is your last chance to have anything that your heart desires! Think about that! What in this world do you really desire?" His voice was smooth and sweet and it sounded like your mother and best friend rolled into one. This was the voice of compassion, offering me anything that my heart had ever desired. Before I could break the spell, Mr. Nelson spoke again. "Now just ask for it and it shall be given!"

It was true, all I had was an old ragged out car and second-hand furniture, all of which would fit in a small U-Haul. Then I remembered that Pam and Michael were sitting in the car waiting for me. I don't know where the next words that came out of my mouth came from, but thank goodness they did, "About the only thing that I have of value is my soul, and I would like to keep it!"

That was the straw that broke the smile on Mr. Nelson's face. I could see the anger building in his face and the cold room made his face seem to glow red! I knew that it was time for me to go before he could say another word, so I reached for the doorknob, opened the door, turned and said, "Thanks for the offer Mr. Nelson, but I have to pass on that one!"

I was out of his apartment door in a flash and pulled it closed behind me. I was running down the hall to the stairs and I could hear Mr. Nelson yelling all the way down the stairs! At times, it didn't even sound like a human yelling. I'm sure the other people in the apartment building could hear Mr. Nelson and wondered what was going on. I was finally out of the front door and running to the side parking lot where our car was parked. I jumped in and started the car.

Pam said, "What happened up there?"

I said, "Mr. Nelson isn't too happy that we're leaving!" I left it at that, and for the most part I never told anyone about my last visit with Mr. Nelson. After all, who would believe me? I wanted to forget about the dreams and the last visit with Mr. Nelson. The next few years of my life was as normal as anybody else, broke and in the army.

The peace in my dreams was good, no matter how short it lasted.

CHAPTER 6
NEW BATTLES

"When darkness is upon your door and you feel like it's a lost battle. You put your defenses down and await the dusk of your life, look beside you and you'll find me with an armor to make sure I die before you fall!"~Rose Hathway

The next several years went by without any really bad dreams for me. My father had fallen sick and the doctors couldn't find the problem. We feared he would not make it. I requested help from our State Senator to see if he could help me get transferred to a base in Georgia where I could go home on weekends and help with my father. I was a good soldier in the Army, but this was a big mistake! The army did not like a letter from a Senator trying to tell them what to do with one of their soldiers! Shortly after, I received a call from the Base Headquarters informing me that I had been discharged from the employment of Uncle Sam and I had one week to check out.

Now I had no job and a wife and two little boys to support. We loaded up and headed back to Tennessee where I found a job working in Cookeville and things were ok. We had purchased a small old house from my father located on his farm. When I wasn't working at the factory, I was working on making repairs to that old house.

My life was about to change and not for the better. One night I heard a noise outside the house so I got up, put my pants on, and walked out of the house. There was a small wet weather spring that ran through a section of the field next to our house. My father had built a small wooden bridge over the stream to make a way to get across the wet areas without stepping in the mud. I could see something standing on the bridge.

It wasn't light, yet it wasn't totally dark outside either. I noticed as I walked, it was as if I was floating across the grass. The air seemed thick, which was odd. I could see currents in the air moving like waves of water. Suddenly, I was at the edge of the bridge. As I stepped onto the bridge I saw there was a man standing hunched over in the middle of the bridge. I could not think of who it would be? Or why someone was standing on the bridge? Even stranger, why was he there? I could not get a good look at him. It was like his form shifted with the current of the wind. I then asked, "Can I help you?"

The man rose from his hunched position and, as he stood upright, his form became clear. This wasn't a man, or a Beast, it was something in-between. I thought this can't be real! But I didn't have time to think anymore because just at that moment it lunged at me. I didn't move fast enough though as I felt the weight of its body as it hit me in the chest. Its weight sent both of us stumbling back and falling on the ground. At this close distance, I could now see that this was more of a Beast than a man.

The Beast had never let go of its grip on me. I looked up I saw red eyes glaring down at me. I didn't see the claw-like hand raised and ready to strike, but a second later I felt a claw tearing at my chest. I could feel my flesh being ripped to shreds. I knew that I was going to lose this fight if I didn't do something fast. Don't ask how, but I managed to throw this thing off of me.

I should have run, but I stood my ground. To think I had a chance in a fight with this thing was crazy. There comes a moment when you have to let go of fear, and reach deep within yourself to find the power to do great things! Even if it means you have to stand your ground with a monster like this. I had been in this spot before and I was tired of running.

The next move I make first and I knocked the Beast off its feet. I never let up and the battle went on for an hour or two. We fought and fought, the Beast tearing at my flesh with it claws and me hitting it with my fists. Once during the fight, I looked down. I was covered in blood. Unfortunately, most of the blood was mine. Some of the blood were the Beast. The entire time the Beast never uttered a word, only grunts and growls.

Finally, we both were so tired that we could barely move, but the Beast made one last move toward me. I managed to side step its charge and pushed the Beast face first to the ground. I jumped on its back and grabbed the Beast around the neck with one arm. I locked my hand in my other arm and pulled with all my strength! I felt something in its neck give. The Beast went still. I sat there for some time too exhausted to even move off the body of the dead Beast. Finally, I stood up and started to walk back to my house when I heard a voice calling me. I turned to see who it was.

"Wayne, Wayne, are you ever going to get up? This is the third time I called for you. If you don't get up, you are going to be late for work!" I knew that was the voice of Pam and I looked around. I was lying in my bed. It had been a dream!

The next night again I heard a noise outside of the house. I found my pants and shirt and pulled them on as I walked out the front door. As I stood on the front porch I could see someone standing on my bridge. I did not realize this was a dream as started walking out to see who there. Just like the night before things seem out of sorts. I didn't really walk but floated across the grass to the edge of the bridge. This time whatever was on the bridge did not wait until I reach the bridge. It was on me in a flash!

I didn't even have time to think about what was happening when suddenly I felt its claws on me. This beast was trying to tear at any part of my body it could reach. I felt my flesh being ripped by small claws that cut like small blades wherever they found skin. This was so unexpected that I had almost lost the battle before I knew it was happening. I had to think fast or it was going to be over for me. I made an attempt to catch one of beast's arms with my hands and by some stroke of luck it worked. I pulled as hard as I could on that arm and at the same time I shoved my shoulder into beast's chest. My face just missed the snapping of teeth, but the move did work.

My blow knocked the breath out of the beast! That gave me the needed time to make one more move. I still had a hold of its arm so I swung it around and the beast went down. The beast was fast, as soon as it hit on its face, it rolled. I then moved and kicked at the same time. Again, I lucked out as my kick caught it in the ribs. I felt something break. I continued to kick and kick! When I finally stopped the Beast did not move. I was completely out of breath. I stood there for some time trying to get my wind back when I started kicking it more. All I could think about was this did not make any sense.

The dreams came almost every night for the next several months. The dreams always started the same, I would hear someone calling me or I would hear a sound outside of the house. I would get up and go outside to see who was calling me or what was making the noise.

Once I woke up hearing the sound of someone crying. I was confused and tired. Some days I would go to work so worn out that I could barely make it through the day. Yet again I climbed out of bed and pulled on my pants and shirt. As I stood on my porch I could see that there was a small boy on the bridge. He was standing in the middle of it and on the other side was a beast.

All I could think was the need to save that small boy! I rushed to reach him before the beast could. The small boy was stooped over crying. I stepped between him and the beast on the side of the bridge. I asked him if he was he all right. I really didn't take the time to look at him as I was watching the beast. He told me he had this dream every night! The monsters would come after him. I told him I would protect him from the monsters.

The beast or monster had not moved until then. It was now starting to walk toward us and then it spoke; "The boy is mine to play with, get out if his dream!" I thought this was strange, how could I be in the boy's dream? I thought this was my dream.

"The boy is not yours, and this is my dream!" I yelled back at the monster.

I was getting better at fighting monsters! In the end, I killed the monster. I walked back to the bridge and looked down at the little boy. He had been so scared that he had not moved during the fighting.

"It's all right now, the monster is gone!" I told him as I reached down and patted his head.

"Are you sure? The monster comes after me every night." He had tears falling from his eyes.

"Yes, and if he does come back, just call my name and I will come and protect you." I told him this, but I wasn't sure I could do that.

He smiled at me and was gone! I slept the rest of the night without any more dreams. Surprising the dreams stopped for a couple of weeks. I was starting to have some hope that it was over, but once again I was wrong.

CHAPTER 7
THE MESSENGER

"Don't blame the messenger because the message is unpleasant."
~ Ken Starr

I had a reprieve from the dreams for a couple of weeks. I thought the dreams were finally gone and was glad. One evening I had a very different dream. I found myself walking down a path in the middle of the woods. I wasn't sure where I was or where I was going. This dream was different from the others as there was the feeling of something very powerful close. The same feeling as when there was a demon around, but different. It was bright, and I could see the sun rays shining through the leaves. Then beams of light were splashing on the ground as I walked down the path. Then I realized I saw in color! This was a great dream. Yes, there were greens, yellows, blues, reds and all other spectra of color. In my previous dreams, everything was gray and dark.

I looked up and there, sitting on a log, was an old man wearing gray clothes. Not jeans, cotton pants and a gray shirt, like scrubs a doctor would have worn in the operating room. I could see his face. He showed a sign of strength and determination. He wasn't old, yet not young either. He was plain looking in some ways, yet I couldn't take my eyes off of him. His hair was gray and brushed straight back, cut above his shoulders. Later I remembered that I hadn't noticed if he was wearing shoes. This was very odd, maybe that's why now I always look at peoples' shoes. As I approached he looked up at me and then stood up and smiled. He was a little taller than I had first thought.

"Welcome Wayne." His voice was very quiet, yet resounded of strength. "I thought it was time we had a talk!"

"You know my name, but I don't think I know you." I said. I had reached the point where I knew the difference between dreams and the real world and this was a dream.

"I have known you for a very long time. Come, sit with me for a while." He made a gesture with his hand for me to sit on the section of the log beside him. Normally, I would not trust anyone in a dream, but I did as he asked without questioning. Maybe that was it; it was not a command.

I walked over and sat down beside the man. "Who are you?"

"Well, let's just say that I'm the one who has been watching over you!" he said with a smile.

"Watching over me, you mean in my dreams?" I wanted him to be clear about this!

"Yes, in your dreams and in the real world too," he said. But before he could say anything else I jumped in.

"What do you mean watching over me?" I found that being direct was the easiest way to get an answer.

"Well, I had been there to help you when you needed it." He said as he looked at me, as if, I should have known about all he had done for me.

"What help?" I asked with a bit of anger in my voice. I had my share of bad luck and, if he had been helping, then why had all these bad things happen to me?

He looked up and said into the air, "Yes, I know this is my task to learn patience."

"OK, who are you talking to?" I was looking up into the air to see if anyone was hiding in the trees. You could never be too careful in a dream.

"Mostly myself, but you never know who is listening. Let me explain some things. We all have jobs to do and my job has been to watch over you. It has been a full time job, I might add. My Lord is very demanding and he doesn't forget our little transgressions you know. So for the little one I made, I got you." He said that as if I would understand that watching me was some type of punishment. There was a smile on his face now.

"You're Lord? Are we talking about the good Lord, you know, the one that rules the heavens?" I had been down this path once before and I wanted to know which Lord we were talking about!

"Yes, he is the good one, as you put it. But if I were you, I wouldn't ever say it quite that way again! Depending on his mood he might not take that remark well." There was true concern in his voice for me. I did not question him as his voice told me that this was not the time to exercise lack of respect.

"OK, if you have been watching over me, what have you ever done for me?" I really wanted to hear him explain this part.

"Well, where should I start? Do you remember the time you threw that piece of metal up in the air and it landed on your head?" He smiled as he said this.

"What do you mean? It busted my head and I still have a dent in the back of my skull over that one." I was thinking how was that helpful?

"Yes, and if I hadn't slowed it down a little, it would have killed you. I broke a couple of rules saving your head on that one. But we both know you have a very hard head!" He wasn't smiling.

"What about the time you fell out of that sycamore tree. Did you stop and think how you landed in the forks and not on the ground?" His voice was a little louder.

"Great job! I was stuck up there for hours! I got in all kinds of trouble from my Mom when I finally made it down!" I wasn't going to let up. That wasn't my idea of help. "Why couldn't you just set me on the ground? What was the point in letting me get stuck up in that tree!"

"The point was you shouldn't have been climbing a tree in the first place. There was a lesson to learn! Not that you learned anything from your mistakes." His voice was rising again. I don't believe he was used to someone questioning him.

"Well, was that all you did for me?" I never know when it's time to count my blessings and shut up.

"What about the car wreck? You were too busy eating chicken and listening to the radio to notice the road!" His voice got even louder this time. "I got into all kinds of trouble on that one! You have no idea how many rules I broke to save you. I had to give an oath that I would never do anything like that again or I would be the one visiting you in your dreams as one of those demons!"

"So that really did happen, I thought I lost my mind or something! So that was what you're doing?" I had to ask.

"Yes, but never again!" His voice had calmed down a little.

"So that was you who folded my clothes on the end of my bed? I always wondered who did that." It was good to know what had really happened even though I didn't know all the details. I decided that I had better not push my luck anymore.

"You mean that after all these years all you are wondering about is who folded your clothes?" He stood up so that I couldn't see his face. I had a feeling it was for the better since he saved my life and all I could wonder about was how my clothes had gotten folded!

Then he turned and I could see the anger in his face! I did not dare speak. He had a look that I may have pushed him to a place I didn't want to go!

"Enough of this! Let me explain the reason I am here. I have a message for you that will help you understand what has been happening." He said this while he was turned away from me so I could not see his face, then he turned and faced me. One look at his face and I knew not to open my mouth again. It was time to sit and listen.

"You have an old soul and old souls like yours have the ability to be aware of what happens in the realms of dreams. Most men do not have this ability. There are demons that have domination over those realms of dreams, but most men never cross their paths."

I interrupted him, "Are there demons that have domination over the waking world?"

"Yes of course, but there are rules. Let's get back to my message for you. Most mortals just dream and because they do not perceive or recognize demons, they are shielded from them by rules. Other mortals, like you, can remember their dreams because they have the ability to cross completely over into that dark world where they interact with spirits both good and bad spirits. Some can protect themselves, others cannot." He hesitated for a moment to collect his thoughts.

"What do you mean that I have an old soul? Are there new souls?" I asked.

"Yes, yes. They told me this wasn't going to be easy!" He made a face like 'Why me?' Then sat back down. "This is going to take a while, I see. Let's try this, I tell you what you need to know, and then you can ask the questions."

"OK, but what's the difference in an old soul and a new soul?" My mind was racing, thinking about the chance to ask all of my questions about the how's and why's! I was thinking of all the other questions I wanted to ask. How was the universe made? How long is a day in God's time frame? What happened in the war between the angels? Had there been more than one war? The questions were endless.

"It's not relevant right now. As I was saying, there has been a shift in power in the world of dreams. Evil has gain power and they are attempting to take over the world of dreams. It's been necessary to have a mortal to balance things." He smiled, because he was able to say all this without my asking a question.

"Why a mortal?" I asked.

He smiled, "That is a good question. As I have said, there are rules that have to be followed. On the other hand, demons don't always follow them or they find a way to bend them whenever possible. Remember, they have dominion over this world. They are still fighting over the fine print of the rules for control of the dream world."

"So you just called me up for this job?"

"Not really, we try to keep a few of the old souls in every generation of man just in case we need them. Some souls will only make one trip down to this world and they reach a level of spiritual understanding and they don't have to return. Others souls take several trips for their spiritual journey. Some souls take a different path; they embrace evil and never return to heaven." I could see he was wondering how much he should tell me.

"How can they do that?" I asked.

"When a baby is born, we send it a soul. Some angels only job is delivering souls." He had that look of envy on his face.

"How does a baby get its soul, I mean, how do you know when it's time?" Once again I asked a question without really thinking.

"That is their job. When a baby takes it first gasp of breath the baby receives its soul. The angels' job is to be there at that moment." He had a funny look on his face like he said something he shouldn't have.

"What do you mean it's their job to be there?" I read more into his answer.

"I didn't want to get into this and I know I already have broken a couple of rules saying what I have. Some answers are not for man's knowledge. I will have to answer for this slip of the tongue, but sometimes an evil soul doesn't return to heaven as I have told you; they stay on in this world. Sometimes they find a baby before we do." He had a sad look on his face.

"So, some people are born evil?" I had a bad feeling with what I had just said.

"Unfortunately, yes. Now we are way off the subject of why I am here. As I was going to say before you asked so many questions, and thought of a million more. Yes, I can see them swirling in your mind! Back to my mission, you have the power to fight evil in the world of dreams. This was given to you long ago. Now you have to help even the balance between good and evil in the world of dreams. Stand up and hold out your hand!"

I jumped up and held out my hand. His voice was so commanding that I did not even question what he had told me to do. I wanted to ask how long ago I got these powers and how? Was this first trip, and if not, how many trips down to earth had I made? I also wanted to ask, why did I have to keep coming back? What was I doing wrong? I had thousands of questions to ask on this subject alone, but his voice was too commanding.

"Now, reach down into yourself, and think of the feeling you have when you are facing a demon. Find that same inner power and then let that feeling grow." I couldn't explain, but I could feel the power rising through my body as I listened to his voice. "Feel that power growing! NOW let it manifest a weapon for you. This is a gift for you."

All of a sudden there was a sword in my hand. I had to ask, "Is this the sword of truth or the sword of power?"

He gave me a disappointed look as he said, "Please get real! This is your weapon, made of your own power and faith. It could have been a shield, a staff, or a club instead of a sword. Your power manifested it in the form of a sword for you to fight against evil. The sword is only as strong as your faith. If your faith is strong enough, then your sword will never fail you." He smiled and started to walk away then he turned and said, "Remember, it is there whenever you need it. Just think about it and you shall have it!"

"Wait, I have more questions!" I started to run to catch up with him. He had been walking only for a second, but he was almost out of sight.

He stopped and turned back to me and said, "I'm sure you do, but I don't have an eternity to spend answering your questions now! Maybe someday!" With that remark, he turned back and was gone. There was a kind of humor in his voice that made me laugh.

Then I heard Pam saying something. "What so funny?" She was looking at me with a question on her face as she woke me. "You were laughing in your sleep."

As I woke up my joy started to leave as I was already missing him. I felt like I had been in a dream with him for years. I couldn't explain it, but I felt completely safe with him. I was so happy! I had forgotten about all my troubles while in this dream. I never felt like that! The moment he left there was sadness starting to fill my heart. As I lay in my bed I started to cry as the happiness had left so fast! It wasn't sadness. It was the lack of goodness! I had lost the feeling that I had never felt before, it was gone.

CHAPTER 8
THE BATTLES RENEW

"Victory occurs when you let God fight your battles". ~ Jim George

It didn't take long for the dreams to ignite. I detected a sound, only this time I wasn't at the house. I was walking on a brick path, and there stood trees growing on each side of the path. In the distance, I could see a small child hugging a tree with a huge monster standing over it. I could hear this child screaming for its life so I started to run, only it seemed like pushing through water. The air was thick and moving was slow and arduous. The distance was short, but it was taking forever to reach this child. This was taking minutes when it should've taken seconds to reach the child.

Before I arrived there, the monster spotted me. This monster was large and moved very quickly for its size. It didn't seem to be affected by the thick air. Once again I had rushed in without thinking and was about to pay the price. I immediately saw the monster was actually a demon running towards me at twice my speed. I knew it would be on me before I could get out of the way.

Too late! It was going fast as a speeding car and I was hit, like a dump truck. I was thrown back onto the brick path. I could feel the hard, rough bricks under my skin. There was no time to consider the pain as the demon was upon me. It seized my body and pulled me up off the brick path only to throw me down again. This time was worse than the first impact because my head hit the brick. Things were starting to get blurry and I realized that the demon was picking me up again.

Panic filled my head and I thought how could I have been so stupid?! After all of these battles, I hadn't learned what not to do! I knew better than to run in without knowing what I was up against. This dream was not going the way it should. Then, in the back of my mind I remembered what I had been told by the messenger. I thought, why didn't he tell me his name? Why didn't I ask his name? I had to remember to ask his name the next time we met. Better yet, why was I thinking about that when I was getting slammed against a brick pathway?

I reached deep within myself and the power began flowing through my body. Just as the demon started to throw me down I found a way to swing around. When the demon threw me down, I planted my feet on the brick path. In my hand was a sword, so I made a swing for the big demon's head. The thick air slowed me down and the demon was able to duck and miss my blow. At least I was now free from its grasp.

The demon could still move twice as fast as I could. The demon's moves were simple and effective! It lurched at my mid-section and took me down to the brick and knocked the breath out of me. Once again, I was not prepared for the attack. I raised the sword and used it to beat the demon any place I could strike a blow. The demon was using its body weight to pound on my chest. With each pounding, my head was hitting the brick I was laying on. My breath was being knocked out with each pounding. Time was running out.

I realized I was losing this battle and had to do something fast. It's funny how thoughts go through your mind at the oddest times. I thought, what would happen if I didn't live through one of these dreams? If I get killed, will I wake up or, would I really die? Hitting this demon with the hilt of my sword was having little effect. I couldn't get in a massive blow and, at best, I was just pounding it in the ribs. I pulled the sword over my head and gripped the hilt with both hands. I knew this was not the best idea, but I had to do something, and do it fast.

The demon raised its body for another blow and I pushed the sword at an angle between me and the demons' chest. The demon was so intent on pounding me that it didn't even see the sword. The demon came down with all its force and impaled itself on the tip of my blade. When the demon realized what happened its red eyes filled with rage and anger. I didn't let go of the hilt as the demon attempted to pull the sword from its chest. I used all my power to thrust the sword deeper. Then the demon gasped for air, its eyes rolled back in its head and fell forward. Its weight was more than I could bear and the hilt of my sword hit me in the chest. I was about to be killed by my own sword.

The weight of the demon was causing the hilt of my sword to put pressure on my chest and break my rib cage. Suddenly the demon was gone! I rolled over grasping for air. My rib cage was hurting so severe that it felt like I had broken several ribs. The air was no longer thick, though it still wasn't easy to catch my breath. I laid there gasping to catch air in my lungs. Ultimately, I could feel my lungs inflating and my breath returning to me. Gradually I stood up and looked around. I wasn't certain how long this fight had been going on? It had seemed like hours, yet it may have only been just a few seconds. In dreams, it's hard to track time. Seconds can seem like hours and hours can seem like seconds.

Then I heard a small voice crying. I had forgotten about the child. I managed to stand and turned to look in the child's direction where he was still sitting in the same spot crying. I gathered myself and walked over to see if he was all right. The air was once again thick. My movement was slow and hard as my strength was all but gone. I could see the air current moving again like waves of water. I thought was strange since usually, these concerns go away once the demons were gone. I knew then that there had to be a second demon around. This fight was not over.

I thought I had better be quick and get the child out of here. I was doing my best to rush to him. I was only a step or two away from his body, when I could hear him cry even louder!

"It's all right, the demon is gone!" My voice seemed strange as the current of the air was distorting it. "We had better leave this place, it is not safe! Hurry, take my hand and I will protect you!" I stretched my hand down to him as I kept watch all around us. I felt the presence of a demon nearby.

Then I felt a grip like a vise on my hand! "You killed my brother!" Its words were loud and full of anger as the current of air made his words even more distorted than mine. The next thing I knew I was being thrown down onto the bricks.

All I could think was not again! The child wasn't that big. I got a closer look under its hood. I could see it wasn't a child, it was a demon. I used my sword to swing at the demon child, but I missed. The demon had to let go of my hand to avoid my blade. I did not waste any time getting to my feet.

Then I heard the voice of a child coming from under the hood saying, "You tried to hurt me! You said you would protect me, didn't you?" The voice of a pleading child stopped me in my tracks. The voice sounded so innocent. What was I doing? Had I gone mad in this dream? My job was to protect children, not hurt them.

Then I could hear the voice of a small child and saw its little hand extended out to me say

"Please give me your hand, I'm so scared!"

I could see a beautiful child standing before me as it reached its hand out to me! "I'm sorry; I don't know what got into me. I'm tired and I know there a demon close to us. We must get out of here!" I reached for the small hand again but just as it touched my hand, I notice a claw opening instead of a small hand. I had been holding my sword up and ready to strike should something jump us. I let the sword fall as the hand gripped my hand. The arm of a small child was cut off. I held the hand and part of the arm in my hand. When I looked down all, I could see was a part of the arm with a claw. The spell was gone and I could clearly see that this wasn't a child, but a demon. The demon was holding where I severed its arm. Clearly it was in pain. It was lost in the moment of looking at its missing arm. That was all I needed for the second blow. It saw my blade falling down on it as it tried to move, but for once, my blade was faster. I hit the demon in the shoulder area and cut through its upper body. The second blow had killed it. The air thickened and the next thing I knew I was sitting up in my bed soaked in sweat.

CHAPTER 9
BETRAYED BY INNOCENCE

"Power corrupts and absolute power corrupts absolutely."
~ Lord Acton

There is an old saying that power corrupts. Too much power leads to arrogance, which leads to your destruction. We all have our moments where we are proudest of ourselves! And we all have moments that we wish we could change forever.

Six months had gone by since I had been granted the knowledge of how to summon my sword of faith. Almost every night I was pulled into the world of dreams because of my calling. I fought and destroyed demons in an effort to balance the world of dreams. They were big, small, smart, and not so smart yet I defeated. The dreams took place almost in the same settings every night. I reached a point where I looked forward to the battles. I must admit I was getting very good at using my sword. I was ready for them bring it on! By this time, I knew every trick possible or so I thought.

One night, I heard a voice calling for help. I realized it was coming from outside my house. In all of the dreams before, I found myself standing on the porch of my house looking out over the field. This one was a little different, though, because I found I was standing out in my yard. There standing on the bridge was a young woman with two demons after her. One demon was on each side of the bridge and she was trapped in the middle. I have learned to proceed with caution, so I did not just rush in as in the past.

Even I can learn from my mistakes if I make enough of them. I have learned that I could not always tell which person was the demon and which was not while I was dreaming. I made my way down to the bridge slowly trying to make sure there were no surprises waiting for me. I confronted the first demon and it did not take much of a battle to dispose of it which should have been a warning. I remember it was large and gray and its body looked like mud. It didn't seem very bright. The woman ran to my side of the bridge as the other demon started to come toward her. I pushed her behind me and I attacked the second demon, which also was as easy to dispose of as the first demon. As I turned to the young woman, I saw that she was crying and I said, "It's all right now, they are gone, you can stop crying!"

With tiny sobs she said, "Thank you, I have been so afraid! They come after me every night in my dreams. This is a dream isn't it?"

Her face was pure and smooth. She had bright green eyes and shoulder length blonde hair which was blowing in the wind. I noticed that there was a soft wind blowing. I could smell the honeysuckles in the air. There were small tears running down her cheeks and I said, "Don't cry, you are safe now!" I stumbled as I tried to walk forward to get closer to her. I looked at her face and it felt like a dream within a dream. I was drawn to her. Something about her looks took my breath away. I got butterflies in my stomach when I attempted to speak to her. I could feel she had an air of innocence about her. The innocence that we all long for as we get older, but is left ever so soon in our life.

"Are you sure they won't come back tonight?" She said as she smiled at me. I could say it was the thought of the demons not coming back that had made her smile, not me. That was fine with me as I knew that in some way I had helped make that smile possible.

She then said, "I don't know why, yet every night they come after me in my dreams. I'm getting to the point that I am afraid to sleep!" She lowered her head and looked down as she spoke to me. There was a sadness that tugged at my heart. I could not explain the sorrow I was feeling just standing there watching and listening to her talk. Her voice was that of innocence to my ears. I couldn't believe that this was happing to me! In all my dreams,

I had never met someone that was so beautiful! And she needed my help. It is necessary to every man to feel needed and we all like to be someone's hero. I reached out to touch her, but she was gone. I woke up a second later in my bed. All I could do was lay there and think about her. It was early in the night yet I could not go back to sleep. Would I see her again? What are the chances of meeting someone in a dream more than once?

The next several nights I did not have any more of these dreams. I could not stop thinking about this girl. Pam seemed to notice that I was lost in thought more than usual. Several times she asked what I was thinking about. I would tell her it was just work. Then I felt guilty that I lied to her. This was crazy, how could someone I met in a dream one time have such an effect on me. I've never been so caught up in the memory from a dream that I could not even sleep. This memory was driving me crazy.

One night I heard someone crying for help! I thought I recognized the voice. I couldn't get my pants and t-shirt on fast enough since all I wanted to do was rush outside. There standing at the edge of the bridge was the young woman. There was a big demon coming after her on the bridge. I rushed to where she was standing and stepped between her and the demon!

The demon roared "Get out of my way, I know of you. I do not fear you! Get out of my way mortal, she is mine tonight!" Its voice carried across the field like thunder. I knew this was going to be a fight. This demon was big and it was smart. I had grown use to fight demons that only had brute strength and no brains, but I could tell this demon had both. I had learned that it was not brute force that won battles; it was who could outsmart their opponent.

"Can you defeat this one or should we run?" the voice from behind me asked.

"Oh, I can take this one!" I told her as I turned and looked at her.

She smiled and said, "Be careful, both of our lives are at stake tonight!" She reached out to touch my face, but just as her hands reached my face, I felt a blow from behind!

I had taken my eyes off the demon and it took full advantage of my mistake to hit me with all its force. As the demon and I went sailing across the field, I managed to push the young woman out of our path. My only saving grace was that the big demon did not manage to get a good hold on me. The big demon had lunged with such speed that as we hit the ground, it landed on the bottom. I heard a groan from beneath me. I was free from its grip. I sprang to my feet, but the demon was just as quick. It was faster than I thought possible. It slashed out with a claw and I felt my chest burn with fire. Now my fighting instincts took over and with my sword in hand, I was fighting back.

This battle was not going to be an easy one. The big demon was quick and for every blow I made he got a blow back. My blows with the sword were cutting deeper than the big demon's claws and this was the only thing that saved me this night. In the end, it was the big demon that lost the fight due to loss of blood from the deep cuts I made with my sword.

As I turned around and faced the girl, she came running to me. She stopped only a foot away and said, "Look at you, you are all cut up and covered with blood. What can I do to help?" Just the sound of her voice made me feel better! Then she said, "I know that there is a spring close by come and I will clean your cuts." She reached and took my hand. It all seemed so natural. I didn't hesitate to let her take my hand in hers. I had learned from my dreams not to let anything take hold of your hand. Or for that matter really touch you.

I broke all the rules and did not even question her. She led me along the path she was taking. I was like a puppy dog being lead to slaughter. My hand in hers made me forget all my problems. It was more than just holding hands, there was something about her that touched my soul. I was lost by the feeling of my hand touching her hand. Even though, there was something going on, I could not explain what.

Shortly, we reached the spring which was coming out of the side of a rock wall. There was some soft green grass where she told me to lie down. She tore off a section of her white dress and dipped it in the spring water and cleaned my cuts. As she cleaned my wounds and continued to wash out the blood from her rag, she talked to me. "You were so brave to fight for me like that! I don't understand what is happening? Why are all these demons after me in my dreams? I have never done anything to cause this. I am so thankful that you found me!" Unlike most dreams where they only last for a few second or so, this one was going on for what could have been hours. I had lost all meaning of time. I had lost myself by just being with her. I thought that I could spend eternity right here at this moment without every regretting a thing.

Her voice was so soft that I forgot I was dreaming. I could feel the gentleness of her hand touch me when she was washing my cuts. With every touch of her skin on mine, I could feel tiny streaks of a warm fire run through my body. It was unlike anything I ever felt. Some ways it felt like real love, and yet in some way it was pure sexual excitement beyond anything I could describe.

"Now, the bleeding has stopped, what shall we do? We have the rest of this dream my hero?" she asked as she looked down at me. She was sitting beside me, and then she started to lean over me. I could feel her soft hair on my face as her lips were just inches from mine. I have never longed to kiss someone in all my life. Her breath was like sweet honey. I could smell it and it had the smell of innocence!

Then she was gone! I awoke back in my bed. As I lay in my bed, all I could think of was her. Even though, we had only been apart for seconds, my heart was broken. It's like a part of me had been torn away. I was no longer complete as the part of me that made me happy was gone. I have never felt loneliness like this before!

The next couple of days was hell. I could not stop thinking about her. And I didn't even know her name. I would have at least had a kiss, if only we had a couple of seconds more! I knew that one kiss would last me a lifetime. Oh, how I longed for that kiss. Every time I thought about that missed kiss it was pure torment.

One whole week went by and still no dreams. This should have been a sign that something was wrong. I couldn't stop thinking about the young woman of my dreams. Then one night I went to sleep, and I found myself walking down a path through some woods. It was a sunny day with a light breeze blowing. All was good! Then I saw something move up ahead on the path. I walked a little faster to see what was there. It was her! She had on a white cotton dress with her shoulder length hair lightly blowing in the breeze. I ran to catch up with her. When she heard me coming toward her, she picked up her pace. I realized that she was afraid of what was going after her.

"It's me, your hero!" I still did not know her name, but I had to let her know it was me.

As she began to move faster, she glanced back to see what was running after her! My heart leaped as I seen her starting to smile. She stopped and turned back toward me and said, "Yes, my hero, you are here in my dream. I had hoped that we would get to see each other again." She smiled as she reached out her hand toward me. I took a step closer and held her hand in mine. We started walking down the path. I didn't know where we were walking, nor did I care as long as I was with her.

She broke the silence by saying, "Isn't it strange that we are together in our dream again?"

"Yes, I didn't think we would see each other again. And there are no demons, or at least for now!" I was so happy just to be with her as we walked together. I don't remember either of us saying a word. We came to the spring that had been in our last dream. We sat down in a soft, fresh grass and talked about the demons.

How they had been in both of our dreams for a long time. She told me that they were always chasing after her. That she did not know what she had done to cause this to happen to her.

I let her talk because I loved to hear her voice. I could have sat there for the rest of my life just listening to her. I know that we had just met, but it's like you wait all your life for that special person to come along and you never really expect to meet that person. Yet here I was with my dream person again. We were sitting on the grass, her blonde hair gently blowing in the wind. She smelled like a fresh fragrant flower.

Suddenly, she stopped talking and leaned into me. We kissed. It was a short kiss, but it was sweet like honey, yet had a hint of fire. We moved back just enough that our lips didn't touch, waiting for the other to make the next move. I could feel her breath on my lips. Then I moved closer until my lips touched hers. There was that taste of honey, then a hint of fire. This sent tingling sensations running through my body which took my breath away.

She pulled back and broke the kiss, "I'm sorry! I shouldn't have kissed you!"

"No, it was OK! No, the kiss was great!" I could not find the right words.

"No, you don't understand, we shouldn't be kissing. I know that you are married! I've seen your wedding band." She looked down at my ring on my finger. "Besides, I shouldn't be feeling anything for you, how do I know you are not evil and tricking me?"

I was so shocked that I did not know how to reply. "I'm not evil; I'm the one who saved you!"

She smiled and melted my heart by saying, "Yes, you did save me. Will you always save me if I need you too?"

I could not get the word "Yes!" out of my mouth fast enough.

She then changed the subject by saying, "You know I don't understand why I'm in this dream? After all, is this my dream or is this your dream?"

Before I could say anything, she was gone. I sat there for several minutes wishing she would come back. Then I woke up! The next couple of days were terrible as I got into a fight with Pam. I could not think of anything but her! And I still did not know her name.

Three nights went by and still no dreams. What they say about the heart growing fonder with absence of the one we love is true. I had to admit that I loved this dream person. And she was ripping my real world apart. Then on the fourth night I found myself walking down the path in the woods again. I recognized this path and knew it led to the spring.

I started to go. There sitting on the grass was my dream girl. When she saw me coming down the path, she smiled. "I couldn't stand not seeing you again," she said as she reached for my hand and pulled me to the grass laughing. "I have to tell you that I'm not quite the innocent girl you think I am!"

I touched her lips with my finger and said, "I don't care." I didn't realize that I had sealed my fate with those three little words.

We started kissing. A burning desire once again raged in my body. We both knew where this was leading! I began to unbutton her white cotton dress. My hands were shaking as I unbuttoned one button at a time. She did not have anything else on under the dress, and with each button opened, more of her body was exposed. After I had released the last button, she stopped me and asked me to remove my clothes.

I could not get out of them quick enough as I was afraid that I would wake up any second. When I removed the last of my close, she reached up and pulled me down on top of her. We made love on the fresh grass. It was more than lust, our souls seemed to touch. We were one in a moment of passion. I could feel sweat run down my back. Had it been minutes or hours? I didn't know as I had never known such passion nor had such a feeling of fire running entirely through my body. The sparks seemed to ignite wherever our skin touched! While I wasn't the most experienced lover, I knew that she had felt it too! We lay beside each other in the sweet grass feeling content and ha

CHAPTER 10
THE FALLEN

"To be a saint is the exception, to sin is to be a man." ~ Victor Hugo

The next night the dreams returned, only things were different. The demons were waiting for me. I had no sword to fight them with. They were strong, and my strength and faith were gone. All I could do was run and hide. It was my fault, the great hero was nothing but a has-been and coward! I had fallen from grace. After several months of nightly dreams being chased by demons, it stopped. I thought they tired of me.

The sad part was I still had feelings for the blond hair woman of my dreams. I hated to think about it, yet it was more than just sex, somehow our souls had touched. I could recognize the evil in her, yet I could also see there was good. Now all I could feel was sadness for her and disgust for me!

One night I found myself back on the path in the woods, only these woods were dead and there were no signs of life. Everything was dying as far as I could see. In Some Way, I felt that it was my fault! The wind was blowing and pushing me down the path. I couldn't stop. I came to the edge of the woods, and all I could see was a wasteland. All living things were gone, the sky was gray, the fields were filled with rocks and broken trees as far as I could see. Death pervaded the land. The wind continued to push me on and there, sitting on a log, was my visitor from dreams long ago.

"Come and sit with me for a while, Wayne." I could hear his voice despite the loud howling of the wind. He was quiet and appeared to be oblivious to the wasteland around us. He gestured for me to come over and sit down. The wind had no effect on him. I made my way over to the log and took a seat beside him.

Once I sat down, all was calm and quiet. The wind did not touch us. I couldn't look him in the face. I held my head down.

"I failed you, I'm sorry!" I said. I wanted to run and hide from him.

"I know what you have done" his words cut all the way into my heart. Yet, there was no bitterness in his voice "That is why I have come to show you something." With those words spoken to me, he stood and motioned for me to follow him. The next second we were standing on a cliff where I could see a rip in the ground. I looked over the opening and saw it was an abyss. When I looked down, I felt myself being pulled in. I began to fall. I could see for miles and miles down into the bottomless pit where there were currents of blackness flowing like a river. It felt as though the abyss was sucking the life out of the world and into the darkness. It seemed to have a life of its own. The abyss was pulling me down into the blackness. His hand grasped me before I had slipped over the side.

"Are you going to cast me into the abyss?" I NIL that's why he brought me here. After all, how could I still have feelings for her, now that I know what she was? I felt that I must have evil in me or how could I care about her?

With a hint of laughter in his voice he said, "No, I want you to see this. Can you see the other edge over there?" He pointed with his free hand and held on to me with the other.

I gazed across the abyss and could see it was a hundred feet or so across and said, "Yes!"

He pulled me back and we were standing in the woods again and they were full of life. He stood looking at me and then said, "I know you've been through a lot. I'm sorry that I couldn't have helped you more, but we all had our part to do! The abyss was ten leagues wide and we had to close it. That's where the demons came from when they opened the abyss. That's why there were so many of them in so many dreams. I don't expect you to understand this, but you were the distraction while we closed that rip. We can never seal it completely, but it had to be closed back to what it is now, manageable."

I looked at him and said, "You mean that all I was just a distraction?" I wasn't even angry at this point.

He smiled again and said, "Yes, they thought that you were the one that could close the rip in the abyss. Someone else took care of that while you were a distraction and a good one at that!"

I looked at him and said, "You know she tricked me! I failed the test! You know what I have done. I still have feelings for her!" I was so ashamed that I couldn't look at him.

"Yes, but what you did was out of love. Besides, you didn't know what she was. My boss wouldn't let me warn you." There was a hint of regret in his voice.

"She took all my power away from me. I have lost my faith!" I said as I had lost all that was dear to me. I hung my head out of shame.

"That was only a deception! She could not take your powers away from you. The only one that could do that was you. Also, you and only you could lose your faith. Remember what I said, the sword is only as strong as your faith. If your faith were strong enough, then your sword would never fail you. They could not take your faith away from you, so they had her trick you into thinking that she could." He reached over and patted me on the shoulder.

"Will I ever get my sword back?" I asked with some glimpse of hope.

"I'm not sure, that depends on whether you can get you faith back" was all he said, but I could read between the lines. He didn't think so, but he didn't want to tell me. Once you have lost such a great gift it not something you are likely to get back.

"I'm exhausted of fighting! I would like for it to stop now, would that be ok?" I asked out of desperation.

Once again he smiled, "I'll see what I can do!" He started to walk away.

I knew that our meeting was over, but I had to ask one more question. "Who are you?"

There was laughter in his voice as he turned and said with a smile, "I am your guardian angel! And don't think it has been an easy job!" I heard laughter as he walked down the path, and as he faded, the dream ended.

He must have changed something because my dreams became ordinary dreams after that night. Once in a while there were dreams where on an occasional demon would show up. I still hated dreams like that, but I cannot help what I dreamed.

Chapter 11
The Return of Two Acquaintances

*"A loyal friend laughs at your jokes when they're not so good,
and sympathizes with your problems when they're not so bad."*
~ Arnold H. Glasgow

Several months had gone by without any dangerous dreams. I was happy to have ordinary dreams again. I assumed the demons got what they needed from me. I had lost my powers, and I really didn't care anymore. My real world life wasn't returning to normal. What I had lost in my dreams had wrecked my real life too, but that's an entirely different story.

As always my dreams happen in secession, the same dream recurring over several nights playing out the full dream. You see, I don't just have one dream on the subject and then never dream about it again. No, my dreams play out like a story.

I began having dreams about being a preacher in a small southern town in the early fifties. The small town had white picket fences that lined the streets. I guess, in some ways, this for me was a dream of redemption. This was a dream that carried me back to a small town in a time where I felt safe. How odd feeling safe to me was living in this small southern town being a preacher. I had on a cool white cotton shirt and light color pants that were appropriate for a summer day. The people in the town were honest and friendly. They would wave at me as I drove through the streets.

Like all dreams, this can be better or worse than real life. I had an old late model forties Chevy, with the gear shifter on the steering column. I remember going down dirt roads, now and then reaching up to speeds of forty or forty-five miles per hour. I could smell the old car's musty odor coming from the cloth seats. I enjoyed that smell as it reminded me of simpler times. My old car was nothing fast or new, but it was great for just putting around the town.

On or about the second night of these dreams I met a woman whose name was Debbie. She had long brown hair and was good looking! She had blue eyes and that shy look you would expect from a woman that you would meet in a church. We dated in my dream and by end of the dream I had asked her to marry me.

During the next couple of dreams, the preparation for the wedding took place. On my wedding day, I found myself standing in front of a small church lined with a white picket fence. The church was a white weatherboard building with two wooden entrance doors. There was a little steeple on top of the church with a cross.

I walked through the gate of the picket fence and onto a rock sidewalk. At the door was an older gentleman wearing a blue suit and tie. He smiled at me and said, "This is a beautiful day to have a wedding. You are a lucky man, preacher!" The next thing I knew I was standing beside him; he took my hand, gave it a long shake, and patted me on the back.

The next thing I remembered was standing in the church watching my bride, dressed in her white gown walking down the aisle. I could see flowers and candles all over the church. People were sitting in the pews. There was a railing between the pulpit and the pews. Debbie, my bride, was escorted by a man whom I assumed was her father (not all things are spelled out in dreams, some just appear). The next thing I knew, Debbie and I were standing together holding hands. I could hear the preacher saying, "If anyone has cause as to why these two fine young folks should not be married, speak now or forever hold your peace."

Suddenly, the doors of the church burst open and strong wind blew through the church. The candles blew out and the flowers began to swirl around the room. Then the sound of the wind turned to howling sounds like animals.

The ground beneath us began to buckle. Suddenly the planks exploded upwards. We were forced apart by flying wood. The flooring in the aisle all of the way back to the doors started to bust apart and planks started flying upward. The guests that were sitting in the pews were screaming as shattered sections of wood were hitting them.

Next, a spirit rose up out of the floor. It was like a cloud of smoke without real form. The only part you could make out was its head, haggard like a very old person. It had long straggly hair and its eyes were red with anger. Its body changed with the shifting of the wind. This spirit looked at me before turning to my bride. Debbie was screaming for me at this point. She stopped screaming when the spirit stopped right in front of her. It began to take on a more substantial form as it started to grow. The spirit became bigger than Debbie. The spirit had opened its mouth and revealed a set of teeth that were as long as swords. Then the spirit let out a roar! I saw Debbie drop to her knees with fear. I jumped between the spirit and Debbie. I was not going to let this spirit harm her.

Debbie grabbed my pant leg and said, "No, it will kill you!"

She didn't want me to give up my life to protect her. At this point, the spirit turned toward me. It started to open its mouth as something inside of me began to change. I felt sadness and joy at the same time. I not sure why but I reached out my hand in front of the spirit. I looked back at Debbie and said, "No, it won't hurt you." I then turned back to the spirit and said, "Why are you doing this?" As I asked, tears began to form in my eyes. I reached out and touched the spirit's face. I heard a gasp from Debbie. The spirit closed its mouth and just floated there.

"How did you know it was me?" the spirit asked, as I had never gotten her name.

"It's hard to say, yet something told me that it was you." I really didn't have an answer on the how, I just knew.

At that moment, I heard a voice behind me say, "You know this, this THING?" Debbie said more as a statement than a question. My bride-to-be's fears now turned to anger!

There are times when a man knows, no matter what he says; it is going to be wrong. "We have met a couple of times before, but it is kind of hard to explain." This wasn't the time to go into details.

"You can't have him!" were the words out of my newly arrived guest's mouth, who's form was now starting to turn into that young lady in a white cotton dress with the green eyes.

Debbie pushed me to one side as she lifted her white gown, and said "If he knows you, then don't worry, I don't want him! He's yours!" With those words, Debbie began to forge her way through the debris and down the aisle of the church. She never looked back as she walked through the doors and out of the church.

"I guess my entrance put a damper on your wedding?" she said with a smile. There wasn't any hiding that she took pride and a lot of joy in what had just happened. She had the look of victory in her eyes.

"I should be angry at you for what you have just done to me!" I said as I turned to face her, "But it wouldn't do any good! I suppose we should get out of here." I took her hand and led her down the aisle attempting not to trip over the broken planks of wood. "I thought there was some kind of rule that your kind could not come into the church?"

"My kind, just what does that mean?" She stopped. I almost fell as it felt like my arm had been attached to an iron statue.

"You know! Your kind; do I have to say it?" I really did not want to say what I was thinking!

"We aren't any different from the other kind; we just choose the wrong side to support in an argument." Then she laughed. "I can't believe you! You think in such simple terms!"

"Yes, yes make fun of me. You appear to be good at that! I'm sure everyone down there had all kinds of laughs about me while you were sitting around the old fire pits." I had to get my cuts in too as we exited the church doors.

"You know, I got in a lot of trouble over you?" There wasn't any laughter in her voice on that statement.

"What, I thought you got some type of medal!" Once again I was saying things that would let some of my anger out, but in ways I didn't really want to hurt her either.

"I got my medal for tricking you! But that's not what I got in trouble for. After it was all over I got in trouble because, well I felt sorry for you. When we were together, that was the first time in a long, long time that someone had seen the good in me! I had forgotten what that was like. You really care for me and that made me feel something for you! I was forbidden to come to you!" She had tears in her eyes.

I reached up and touched her face to wipe the tears away. When my hand touched her face, all those feelings came flooding back. I had not forgotten all she had done to me or what she really was. But I still cared for her. "What an unfortunate couple we make!" was all I said to her.

"I will get into all kinds of trouble for this but my father will forgive me because he does love me! I broke up your wedding! I will tell him that. I did it as a way to torment you! He will take pride that his daughter is spiteful and ruthless just like him. I will tell him that I couldn't stand the thought of you being happy. I'm brave enough to break a few rules to cause you grief. He will forgive me then but will you?" she had to ask.

"Yes, I will forgive you!" was all I said. Then I couldn't help myself, so I had to ask. "What about us? Will we ever be together again?" She smiled and then looked sad. "You don't belong with me. I won't ask you to give up what it would take for you to come with me. I can't go with you, even if I wanted to!"

"I guess we are an odd couple, a little good and a little evil. I'm not sure which is which?" I was trying to make a joke to keep things from getting too anxious. We both knew it was the sad truth that this was not a match made in heaven.

"I know you don't believe me, but you are one of the good souls!" She smiled and reached out her hand to touch my face, but before she made contact with my cheek she was gone! I woke up to both sadness and a bit of joy.

A couple of nights later I had a visitor in one of my dreams. I found myself walking down that same old path in the woods. There sitting on the log was my guardian angel.

"Wayne, come and sit with me for a while!" he said as he waved his hand.

"Well, I guess you are back to tell me that I did wrong again?" I took a seat on the log next to him and was ready to be condemned for having feelings for her.

"What do you mean?" There was a smile on his face this time and joy in his voice.

"I'm sure you know about the wedding and who showed up? I didn't try to hurt her or anything like that. Actually, I forgave her! I still have feelings for her." I knew I was in trouble because every time he showed up it meant trouble.

"I resent that. It's not troubling every time I show up." He scolded me, but not in a mean way.

"It's not fair for you to read my mind after all this is my dream isn't it?" I was never sure whose dream it was.

"No, you are right, but I couldn't help myself. What I came to tell you was that you have found something crucial! You have found compassion and the ability to forgive!" He had a big smile on his face as he reached over and patted me on my back.

"I'm not in trouble for having feelings for her, even if she is a well, you know what she is? Do you understand what I am trying to ask?" I wasn't sure I wanted to put it into words.

"Well, thank goodness I can read your mind! It's OK, you can see all that is evil in her and yet you still see the goodness in her. Once, a long time ago there was only goodness in her. You have seen that part of her again. That is the power you now have, to look past the bad and evil, to see the good!" That was all he said.

"Is there any hope for her, could she come back?" I wasn't sure he understood what I was asking, because he didn't speak for a long time. "That's not up to me, but I'm afraid my boss is not quite as forgiving as you are when it comes to us!" He had a smile on his face as he said that.

"Well, what about me?" I asked because he was standing up which meant that he was getting ready to leave.

"That is between you and the boss! Oh! I have a new assignment now. The boss doesn't think you will need my help that much now! But, I will still be around to keep an eye on you, just in case!" With that, he was gone!

He has never come back to see me, nor has she.

It ended that night. Most of my dreams have been as ordinary as dreams can be. I do have scary dreams every now and then. At times, I still find myself fighting battles with demons in my dreams. I was given something grand, but I couldn't hold onto. I readily deceived. I still feel the shame of what I have done after all these years. I have forgiven her long ago, just not myself. All this has left its mark on me. I can see spirits now, they are drawn to me. I don't understand why. Sometimes I still feel the presence of evil spirits. When that happens, I try to avoid them. Believe me they are out there.

Epilogue

*"To a people ... who ... believe in genii, ghosts, goblins, and those terrific things that 'go bump in the night', protective charms are eagerly sought for." - 1918 B*ulletin of the School Oriental and African Studies:

I understand that are those that do not believe in demons and spirits. Believe sometime only come when one as been there. I have been there and I know what it's like to stand toe to toe with a demon. There are things that I have done that no one should have done. And I have been to places that no man should have gone. None of this made me a better person. And I did not gain the answers to many of the questions that we want to ask. My dreams too into those places no man should go and I was just luckily to come back home.

I now know that real demons exist in this world and in the world of dreams. Some will believe this is just another story with. What I can say, I was there. I have seen things that very few ever seen and done things that very few have every done. I'm not proud of all my actions in the world of dreams. I did not survive without scars. They are the scars that you can't see from the outside but the scars are real. You can't step into the world of good and evil and not be changed. You may think that I would become religious or a devout person. It didn't happen to me. Maybe I did not go that way because I never forgave myself completely. The scars, at least to me, are what some would call a blessing, but again I do not see it that way either.

I can feel the present of evil at times. I look at this ability as a curse. Plain and simple, there is nothing blessed about that. Also, I see spirits and/or ghosts now. After all these years, I have gotten used to I that curse and will carried it with me to the end of my days. I don't look for them, it seems that at times they seek me out. I think that they realize that I can see them too. Most spirits are not bad, mostly they are confused. They are lost and if even for only a second to have someone see them and know they exist is comforting to them. Again, I cannot say for sure, it's just the look on their face. Most of the time contact happens when I'm least expecting it. It's not something that I can do all the time. And to be honest I do not really care for this curse. Not all ghosts are good; some are evil or bad tempered. I hide this most of the time as many people would think I was just crazy or weird.

This is my story and there are things that I have forgotten or did not bother to tell. When things go bump in the middle of the night, you may not want to go and see what it is. And remember may have been more than just a bad dream!